M000158137

Resurrected to Eternal Life

Resurrected to Eternal Life

On Dying and Rising

JÜRGEN MOLTMANN

TRANSLATED BY ELLEN YUTZY GLEBE

FORTRESS PRESS
MINNEAPOLIS

RESURRECTED TO ETERNAL LIFE
On Dying and Rising

Translated by Ellen Yutzy Glebe from the German *Auferstanden in das ewige Leben: Über das Sterben und Erwachen einer lebendigen Seele* (Gütersloher Verlagshaus, 2020)

Unless otherwise noted, Scripture quotations are from the New Revised Standard Version of the Bible, copyright © 1989 by the Division of Christian Education of the National Council of the Churches of Christ in the USA and used by permission. All rights reserved.

Scripture quotations marked (KJV) are from the King James Version.

Cover design: Brice Hemmer

Print ISBN: 978-1-5064-6939-3
eBook ISBN: 978-1-5064-6940-9

Contents

Foreword

Since publishing my book *Theology of Hope* in 1964 (English edition, 1967), I have often addressed the significance of Christ's resurrection for our lives in this world and our hope for eternal life in the world to come in theological terms—for example, in my short book entitled *In the End—the Beginning: The Life of Hope*, published in 1995 in German and in 2004 in English translation. When my wife, Elisabeth, died in 2016, however, my perspective on these matters became intensely personal, and I was forced to rethink my theological position.

This work does not aim to outline an *ars moriendi* (i.e., to prepare the reader to die) but rather to prepare the reader for resurrection in the fullness of life that we call eternal life—an *ars resurgendi*. We can only practice the *ars moriendi* once, whereas we can practice the *ars resurgendi* throughout all the life we live. Every new beginning is a "resurrection." With this book, I aim to provide comfort and hope, and a sense of assurance, for memorial services. By presenting my thoughts in the form of an essay, I have combined personal stories and biblical witness with my own experiences, something that is not possible in an academic format. This is not intended as a work of scholarship, which is why I have refrained from the use of theological jargon and extensive footnotes.

I have tried to learn what grief is. I have tried to learn what shared happiness is, happiness that does not fade, and I have tried to imagine what it is like for our entire lived lives to be reawakened after death. I have pondered the death and reawakening of a living soul. We die into the resurrection, and the eternal life is the life of the world to come.

Jürgen Moltmann
Tübingen, Easter 2019

1

Two Questions

IS THERE LIFE AFTER DEATH?

After Whose Death?

Many of those who ask the question of whether there is life after death think instinctively of their own death. What comes after death, if anything? When asking this question, it is important to realize that we do not experience our own death. We experience our own dying but not our own death. Strictly speaking, we cannot even say that those who have died are "dead" but rather only that they have died. No one has ever experienced their own death, for even near-death experiences are part of life *before* death.

The same can be said of the "nothing" that many people expect to find after death: no one has ever seen it.

But what about life after the death of others in our lives? Is there life after the death of a beloved child or a cherished partner?

For many people, this is an essential life question. We experience our own dying but not our death. It is only when loved ones die that we experience death. We experience their death through our love for them and their lives.

How are we to go on living after this love has died? How are we to live this life without them? What is the outlook for those "left behind," for those from whom the death of a loved one has robbed any joie de vivre—and often even the will to live? This is a true death experience.

It helps those of us left behind to go on living after the death of our loved ones if we can believe in and sense their secondary presence in the unseen world that surrounds the world we see. This does not, however, alleviate our grief, which is as deep as our love was. Grief is more than self-pity; self-pity has no place in mourning the loss of a loved one. In our grief, our loved ones are with us. This is why our grief "never ends," as Paul writes of love. Is our love for the dear one who has died "as strong as death," as the Song of Solomon claims? Or is death in fact stronger than mortal love?

The joy of love transcends the death of a loved one, for in the joy of love we hear echoes of eternal life. Goethe knew this when he wrote, "Yet, to be loved, what happiness! What happiness, ye gods, to love!"[1]

And believers know the following:

Where true charity and love abide, God is dwelling there—

Ubi caritas et amor, Deus ibi est.

(ELW 642)

Our mortal love of those we cherish is an echo of the divine love, and in love's happiness lies a spark of divine joy.

ETERNAL LIFE: WHAT ARE WE ASKING?

Before we can try to answer the question, we must be more specific about what we mean and narrow our focus.

Eternal life cannot seriously mean the infinite extension of this life. Advances in modern medicine and genetic engineering have nothing to do with the religious concept of eternal

---

1   Johann Wolfgang von Goethe, "Welcome and Farewell," in *Selected Poems*, ed. and trans. Christopher Middleton, vol. 1 (Princeton, NJ: Princeton University Press, 1994), 11.

life, for eternity is not the same as infinity. The immortality for which so-called transhumanists strive would be the end of mankind. An endless life of the sort we have here in this world would be meaningless and terribly boring.

Neither should eternal life be equated with the immortalization of an individual's short life. The way obituaries sometimes speak of the deceased being immortalized is evidence of this folly. For, in that case, we could expect nothing new of eternity but rather only the end of this life and—as it is often called—eternal rest. But is eternal rest something other than eternal death?

It helps if we speak of an eternal liveliness rather than an eternal life; this shifts the focus to the intensity rather than the longevity of the experience. It is not the temporal length of life but the momentary depth of our experience that comes close to the primacy of that which we call "eternity."

Chronological time has nothing to do with this eternity of experience but rather only with the dying of life. A moment of true contentment is like an atom of eternity, and its light is like a flicker of the eternal light. When we are happy, we say that "time stands still." It is love that makes life lively and sparks our joy in living. The delight we take in loving and living leads us to seek the fullness of life and call it eternal life.

Our lives here and now are in the temporal realm. When we look to the past, we speak of how time is fleeting. When we look to our death, we are focused on our own mortality as the limitation of our "life-time." But temporal life is in every instant nascent life as long as we look to the future and remain conscious of our birth. Every moment in time is the beginning of the future, and the past is the future that is now behind us. Just as birth precedes death, the future precedes the past.

The fleeting moments of the past have been consigned to death, while nascent time is a life blessed with a future. If we look beyond the dark horizon of death through to the dawn of God's new day, it is the nascence of all those things we love that fill us with life. We greet each and every new morning in the light of that "bright and morning star" as the hymn proclaims, an eternal dawn. The liveliness of this beginning promises a life fulfilled. We experience life with a sense of fulfillment when that life is at one with itself and pervaded by an affirmation of life that nips the poison of negativity in the bud. It must be a life in the eternal present without dwelling on what was or what is not yet. It must be a life in the here and now, without missing out on life or getting lost in one's visions of what could be. Humans have sought this experience in the mystical *nunc aeternum*—the eternal moment—and found it in silence.

2

The Resurrection of Jesus Christ

It is only because the women who had been close disciples of Jesus and the apostles encountered Jesus after his death that we know anything of Christ. If not for these "postmortem" experiences with Jesus, there would be no Christianity. The Christian faith can thus be seen to have its very origin in the event that the apostles and these women called "Christ's resurrection from the dead." It happened to Jesus of Nazareth, who had died and been buried; his "resurrection from the dead" lifted him up in their eyes as the "Son of God," as Paul writes in an early Christian confession of faith (Rom 1:4). They remembered the story of Jesus in the light of his resurrection, and they told and proclaimed it as a story of Christ, relevant for their age. They hoped to be woken to eternal life along with Christ, and they conceived of their lives in the fellowship of Christ as bringing them into the new creation of the world (2 Cor 5:17). How did this happen? What was "the resurrection of Jesus Christ from the dead" and what does it mean for us? What are its consequences for our own lives and our own dying?

1. THE HOPE OF THE APOSTLES CRUCIFIED

The Gospels provide ample testimony to the apostles' flight from the crucifixion and Peter's denial of his master. The story of Gethsemane is the key to what happened to Jesus and the apostles at Golgotha. Jesus's prayer to "Abba, Father" to "remove this cup from me" goes unheard (Mark 14:36). Jesus dies having been forsaken by God. With his last breath, he asks, "My God, my God, why have you forsaken me?" (Mark 15:34). Judas "betrays" him to the Romans (Mark 14:44); Peter, who had been the first to confess that Jesus was Christ (Mark 8:29), denies him three times (Mark 14:66–72); all the apostles leave him and flee. Jesus dies a lonely death on a Roman cross, condemned as a "terrorist" against the Roman Empire. There was no miracle. He died helplessly. *Betrayed, denied, abandoned.* Those are not just words of mortal weakness and infidelity; they reflect a deep sense of disappointment.

When Jesus had entered Jerusalem, the oppressed had cried out, "Blessed is the coming kingdom of our ancestor David!" (Mark 11:10). "But we had hoped that he was the one to redeem Israel," lamented the disciples on the road to Emmaus (Luke 24:21). For those who had left everything to follow Jesus, who harbored messianic hopes for the liberation of Israel from Roman occupation and the restoration of David's kingdom, Jesus's powerlessness and God's silence at Golgotha were bitter disappointments. They betrayed, denied, and abandoned him, for he had betrayed, denied, and abandoned them. Jesus's crucifixion and God's silence put an end to their hopes in him. They turned back to Galilee from whence they had come and returned to their work as fishermen.

2. THE WOMEN'S FAITH IN THE WORLD DESTROYED

While the men who followed Jesus fled, the women steadfastly accompanied him to his death and watched "from a distance." In other words, they maintained eye contact with their friend. These women are named in the Gospels (e.g., Mark 15:40). They were not alienated by death, and it could not disrupt their love for Jesus. When Shabbat was over, Mary Magdalene, Mary the mother of James, and Salome went to their friend's grave and heard the voice of an angel: "He has been raised; he is not here" (Mark 16:6). It was only before the empty tomb that they succumbed to fear and trembled.

In front of the empty tomb, there was no Easter joy but only unspeakable dismay. Like birth, death is part of our finite, mortal existence. Trusting in the natural course of life includes trusting in death. "We all have to die once," people say. What shocked the women as they stood before the empty tomb and heard the voice of the angel was the collapse of this natural order of life and death. If death is no longer certain, we can no longer be certain that the deceased are truly dead. From its inception, the mystery of Jesus's resurrection was terrifying—a mysterium tremendum. The conclusion of the Gospel of Mark provides ample evidence of this.

3. MARY MAGDALENE

Of all the apostles and Jesus's disciples, the one who was closest to Jesus was a woman named Mary, who came from the village of Magdala on the Sea of Galilee. As a result of the closeness of their relationship, men have sought to discredit Mary Magdalene and any memory of her from the very beginning. To this end, the church fathers equated her with the "sinful woman" (Luke 7), and noncanonical texts of early Christianity—and even modern historical fantasy novels—sought to dismiss her relationship to Jesus as (merely) romantic.

Pope Gregory I preached in 597 CE, "She whom Luke calls the sinful woman, whom John calls Mary, we believe to be the Mary from whom seven demons were ejected according to Mark. And what did these seven demons signify if not all the vices? It is clear, brothers, that the woman previously used the unguent to perfume her flesh in forbidden acts."[1]

The pope thereby conflated four different stories about four different women and attributed all the negative aspects of them to Mary from Magdala. It was only the Second Vatican Council in 1965 that corrected this image, and in 2016, Pope Francis honored Mary Magdalene with a formal feast day, thus setting her equal with the male apostles. Even today, however, she remains the object of men's sexual fantasies, this *magna peccatrix*, the great sinner, a prostitute, devastated by her own vices. The "seven demons" from which Jesus healed her were equated with the "seven deadly sins." There is a long tradition of images of the crucifixion depicting her embracing the cross, her long hair flowing about her.

The attempts to discredit Mary began in the Gospel of John: Peter and the other apostles did not believe her when she told them that the tomb was empty. The disciples raced to the open tomb to see for themselves (John 20:1–10). In the Gnostic gospels, which were not included in the canon, Peter is reported to have said, "Make Mary leave us, for females are not worthy of life."[2] Nevertheless, Peter asks Mary to share with him and the other apostles that which the Savior had revealed exclusively to her, whom he loved more than the other women. When Mary describes a conversation she had had with Jesus about a vision in a dream, Peter is incredulous: "Has the Saviour spoken secretly to a woman and not openly so that we would all hear?"[3]

---

1   Cited from Bonnie Ring, *Women Who Knew Jesus* (Ishpeming, MI: BookVenture, 2017), 265.

2   Elaine Pagels, *Beyond Belief: The Secret Gospel of Thomas* (New York: Random House, 2003), 241.

3   Karen L. King, *The Gospel of Mary of Magdala: Jesus and the First Woman Apostle* (Santa Rosa, CA: Polebridge Press, 2003), 17.

This suggests an open rivalry between Peter and Mary of Magdala in the first congregation. The apostles found this woman to be disconcerting: "My Lord," Peter says in the *Pistis Sophia*, another apocryphal text, "we will not endure this woman, for she taketh the opportunity from us and hath let none of us speak, but she discourseth many times."[4] Is Paul's instruction that "women should be silent in the churches" directed toward her?

Who Was the Mary from Magdala in the Bible?

Mary of Magdala was present at Jesus's crucifixion and death, she was there when his corpse was laid in the tomb, and she was the first person to behold the empty tomb and the resurrected Jesus. She is the perfect witness of Jesus's death and resurrection.

According to Luke, Jesus had healed her of "seven demons," after which she followed him like the apostles. The Gospels of Matthew and John do not mention her illness—neither do the apocryphal texts. I assume that having been healed, she followed Jesus and was enthusiastic about his gospel message. Luke presumably added the "seven demons" in order to be more specific about the "evil spirits" his account mentions (Luke 8:2). Mary was the first member of the group of women who became literal followers of Jesus, and she is consistently the first one mentioned. Apparently, she was the group's representative.

Unlike the apostles, who flee, and Peter, who denies his association with Jesus, Mary Magdalene watches "from a distance" as Jesus is crucified. She accompanies him to his death (Mark 15:40; Matt 27:56; John 19:25). She also goes with Joseph of Arimathea, to whom Pilate releases the corpse for burial (Mark 15:47), and she visits the tomb after the Sabbath to anoint the corpse as was customary in Israel. Thirty-six hours after Mary had seen Jesus die on the cross and his corpse placed in a tomb, she found the same tomb empty.

4   G. R. S. Mead, trans., *Pistis Sophia: A Gnostic Gospel* (San Diego: Book Tree, 2006), 47.

The original text of the Gospel of Mark ends here: "So they went out and fled from the tomb, for terror and amazement had seized them; and they said nothing to anyone, for they were afraid" (Mark 16:8). The text that was later added was inspired by the other Gospel accounts. In Matthew's version, an "angel of the Lord" wearing robes as "white as snow" proclaims, "Do not be afraid; I know that you are looking for Jesus who was crucified. He is not here; for he has been raised, as he said. Come, see the place where he lay. Then go quickly and tell his disciples, 'He has been raised from the dead, and indeed he is going ahead of you to Galilee; there you will see him.' This is my message for you." (Matt 28:5–7).

According to Matthew, the women left the empty tomb with "fear and great joy" (Matt 28:8).

The evangelist John painted the picture of Mary Magdalene's encounter with the resurrected Christ in such a way as to emphasize the depth of their relationship but also Jesus's farewell:

> But Mary stood weeping outside the tomb. . . . "They have taken away my Lord, and I do not know where they have laid him." When she had said this, she turned around and saw Jesus standing there. . . . Jesus said to her, "Mary!" She turned and said to him in Hebrew, "Rabbouni!" (which means Teacher). Jesus said to her, "Do not hold on to me, because I have not yet ascended to the Father. But go to my brothers and say to them, 'I am ascending to my Father and your Father, to my God and your God.'" Mary Magdalene went and announced to the disciples, "I have seen the Lord"; and she told them that he had said these things to her. (John 20:11–18)

Here, in front of the empty tomb, Mary cannot find the corpse of her friend. That is why she is weeping. The one whom she meets here is not the resurrected Jesus but the ascending Jesus: he is still on the way from the realm of the dead to his "Father" and "God" in heaven. He spends forty days on earth in order to reveal his resurrection. And he invites the apostles and Mary into his own relationship to God: my father is your father, my God is your God.

Noli me tangere: it is not clear why Jesus denies Mary physical contact when he permits the "doubting Thomas" to touch the scars from his crucifixion. The theologian Elisabeth Moltmann-Wendel considered what that meant to Mary:

> Mary Magdalene experienced physical salvation in a way which went beyond almost everyone else. She loved Jesus personally. . . . She never doubted him. But now she begins to cling to him. It is not the dead Messiah which makes her doubt, but the lost body of Jesus. It is here that she experiences death; here her existence falls apart. I would prefer to translate the words "Don't touch me" like this: "Grow up, be mature! Accept the grief of parting." "Why do you seek the living among the dead?," the angel asks the women in the Gospel of Luke. The voice is still near and familiar, and in this voice Jesus is still the same. With this voice he gives her a task which does not do away with the distance now between them, but makes it comprehensible: his God is also the God of them all. His Father is also the Father of them all.[5]

Mary did not only "see" the ascending Jesus; he also spoke with her and instructed her as an apostle to proclaim God's message. She was thereby made, in the words of the early church, into an "Apostle to the Apostles." Her friendship with the mortal Jesus evolved into a divine fellowship with the resurrected Christ. Mary was the last person who saw Jesus among the living, and she is the first person who saw him in the postresurrection world. She looked him in the eyes and heard his voice. She carried out the task given her and thereby became the mediator of the new fellowship of those who believed in Christ.[6]

5   Elisabeth Moltmann-Wendel, *The Women around Jesus* (New York: Crossroad, 1990), 71–72, http://archive.org/details/womenaroundjesus0000unse.

6   Ring, *Women Who Knew Jesus*, 181–93.

Mary of Magdala belongs in the center of the church, not just Mary, Jesus's mother, who was skeptical about the movement surrounding her son (Mark 3:21) and only later became part of the first congregation. Throughout the entirety of Christian history, there has indeed been a tradition of honoring Mary Magdalene, as Moltmann-Wendel has shown. Michelangelo's masterpiece, the *Pietà*, depicts a woman so young that it could well be Mary Magdalene.

4. THE NEW REALITY OF JESUS CHRIST'S RESURRECTION

Any study of the Easter accounts of the apostles in Galilee and the women in Jerusalem shows the unprecedented nature of the new reality in which Jesus "appeared" after dying on the cross and being placed in the tomb. This was no reanimation of a dead person, but the apostles and the women initially failed to understand this new reality. Jesus "showed himself" or was "revealed" to them; it was only then that they recognized the apparition. This recognition was tied to the scars from the crucifixion, the familiar ritual of breaking bread together, and his voice. As soon as the disciples in Emmaus "saw" him, Jesus "vanished from their sight" (Luke 24:31). He appeared to them "in another form" (Mark 16:12). These "apparitions" are met with disbelief, not with faith (Mark 16:11, 13, 14); the apostles were overcome with doubt, as related in the story of doubting Thomas (John 20:24–29). It was the apparition of Christ that admonished them to believe, gave them peace, and breathed on them with the Spirit of the resurrection (John 20:22).

No one saw what had happened to the dead Jesus. They only had their impressions of his death on the cross, his placement in the tomb, and his appearances before them as "the living [Christ]." From the very beginning, they did not consider the possibility of his having avoided death like Elijah or Enoch, who were taken up directly into heaven. From the very beginning, they spoke of Jesus's having been "woken *from the dead*."

According to the prophetic eschatology of that period, there was an expectation of a general awakening of the dead.

Paul too viewed what happened to Jesus after his death through the prism of this general expectation for the dead to be raised: "If there is no resurrection of the dead, then Christ has not been raised" (1 Cor 15:13). The apostles and the women, however, spoke of Christ, who had risen "from" the dead. Such exceptions were not foreseen in the prophetic expectations, and it was not considered an exception but rather the beginning of the general resurrection of the dead. Christ was the "first of the deceased" and the "instigator of life." In the resurrected Christ, the apostles and the women got a glimpse of eternal life: "We declare to you what was from the beginning, what we have heard, what we have seen with our eyes, what we have looked at and touched with our hands, concerning the word of life—this life was revealed, and we have seen it and testify to it, and declare to you the eternal life that was with the Father and was revealed to us" (1 John 1:1–2).

5. OVERCOMING DEATH

Jesus's resurrection from the dead was never viewed as an individual resurrection but rather as universal as death is for mortal man: "For as all die in Adam, so all will be made alive in Christ" (1 Cor 15:22). The Pascha (Easter) icons of the Orthodox tradition show this: the resurrected Christ takes Adam's hand with his right hand and Eve's hand with his left hand to pull both up from their graves. With Adam and Eve, Christ pulls all of humanity from the "kingdom of death" into the light of eternal life. Christ's death on the cross was lonely, and his experience alone; his resurrection is a collective, inclusive act that encompasses all of humankind and all of creation—a cosmic event, the beginning of a new creation of all things.

The "resurrection from the dead" is the mortal side of the resurrection of Jesus Christ; the new creation of all things in "the life of the world to come," as the Nicene Creed puts it, is the cosmic side: "He will swallow up death forever" (Isa 25:8); "Death will be no more" (Rev 21:4).

In the words of Paul, "the last enemy to be destroyed is death" (1 Cor 15:26). He rejoices: "Where, O death, is your victory? . . . But thanks be to God, who gives us the victory through our Lord Jesus Christ" (1 Cor 15:55, 57). That from which the women fled, terrified, becomes a reason for the first Christians to celebrate: the world of life without death and destruction. This is incomprehensible and unimaginable given established rational expectations. Something that is impossible in this finite world becomes reality in God's new world. This is why Christ's resurrection is often compared to creation: Christ is the "new Adam." Celsus, an opponent of Christianity in the second century, accused Christians of upending the natural order of the world and of fostering a "world revolution." This is also reflected in the "anarchic" prophecies of the apostle Paul: "Then comes the end, when he hands over the kingdom to God the Father, after he has destroyed every ruler and every authority and power" (1 Cor 15:24). In Christians' eyes, the resurrected Christ became a force of protest against the godless powers and authorities that are deadly for humanity and the earth. This destruction of trust in the world's natural order of death is transformed into the celebration of the new creation. The despair over the injustice of this world is transformed into a certainty in the victory of divine justice in the world to come, the world that begins with Christ's resurrection. In the light of Jesus Christ's resurrection, it becomes possible for life to overcome death, justice to overcome violence, and creation of being to overcome destruction. The force that woke Christ from the dead is the divine force of creation, just as potent as on the first day of creation.

6. CHRIST'S DESCENT TO HELL

> Do not be afraid; I am the first and the last, and the living one.
> I was dead, and see, I am alive forever and ever; and I have the
> keys of Death and of Hades. (Rev 1:17–18)

With these words, the author of the book of Revelation sums up the mystery of the resurrected Christ. Christ himself is the key to the kingdom of the dead, for "he was dead and lives in eternity." Can the same be said for hell, that place where the damned reside? Jesus was damned and is chosen. Did Christ's descent into hell come *before* his death, between Gethsemane and Golgotha, as Luther and Calvin believed, or did it come after his death on the cross and before his resurrection, as expressed in the Apostolic Creed? These two accounts do not stand in opposition: because Christ experienced the despair of the damned in having been abandoned by God between Gethsemane and Golgatha, he has the key to the hell of the damned—he himself is the key to hell. Paul even writes of Christ's "becoming a curse for us" (Gal 3:13). Just as he obliterates the kingdom of death with his resurrection, he knocks down the gates of hell with the cross. There is no other revelation of hell aside from Christ's descent to the netherworld. Luther convincingly suggested the following in his "Sermon on Preparing to Die" (1519): "You must not regard hell and eternal pain in relation to predestination, not in yourself, or in itself, or in those who are damned. . . . Gaze at the heavenly picture of Christ, who descended into hell [1 Pet 3:19] for your sake and was forsaken by God as one eternally damned when he spoke the words on the cross, . . . 'My God, my God, why hast thou forsaken me?' [Matt 27:46]. In that picture your hell is defeated and your uncertain election is made sure. . . . Seek yourself only in Christ and not in yourself and you will find yourself in him eternally."[7]

7   Martin Luther, "A Sermon on Preparing to Die (1519)," in *Devotional Writings*, ed. Martin O. Dietrich and Helmut T. Lehmann, trans. Martin H. Bertram, vol. 1, Luther's Works 42 (Minneapolis: Fortress, 1969), 105–6.

Christ descends into hell in order to throw open its gate:

> The gates of hell He hath laid low,
> And loosed the captives from the foe,
> Now from eternal death we go![8]

The purpose of Christ's descent into hell is that he is with us when we endure hellish misery. Christ—who himself experienced being abandoned by God—is there when we feel abandoned ourselves, be it in that "dark night of the soul" or in physical torture:

> Now I will cling forever
> To Christ, my Savior true;
> My Lord will leave me never,
> Whate'er He passes through.
> He rends death's iron chain;
> He breaks through sin and pain;
> He shatters hell's dark thrall;
> I follow Him through all.

(ELW 378)

Does this provide comfort in those hells that humans create for their fellow beings? Who can imagine the hell in the screams of the dying in the gas chambers of Auschwitz?

Since Christ's descent into hell, there is hope even where all hope has vanished: the hope for the resurrection of the murdered. When I visited what is left of the death camp Majdanek near Lublin, Poland, in 1961, I imagined I could see them, the resurrected Jewish children who had been murdered there, coming toward me in the fog.

---

8   Matthew Carver, "Wir Wollen Alle Fröhlich Sein," HYMNOGLYPT (blog), April 25, 2014, http://matthaeusglyptes.blogspot.com/2014/04/wir-wollen-alle-frohlich-sein.html.

7. THE PASSION OF CHRIST IN THE LIGHT OF HIS RESURRECTION

[Jesus our Lord] was handed over to death for our trespasses and was raised for our justification. (Rom 4:25)

This is how Paul describes the salvation that manifested in the death and resurrection of Jesus Christ. Sin is godlessness, and godlessness leads to godforsakenness, regardless of whether or not one conceives of the latter as a punishment. Sin is not to be understood as the moral equivalent of "guilt." Sin is the distancing of oneself from God and from the life that he offers each individual. Sin is deeper than guilt. Guilt stems from infringing upon our relationships with others. Sin is an infringement upon our relationship to God. Sin thus touches upon the very foundation of human existence. Sin is a "sickness unto death," to use Kierkegaard's definition. The sinner finds himself without or outside of God. In the language of the Bible, this is the "kingdom of darkness." Sin results not only in death but also in "degeneracy."

The divine judgment meted out for mortal godlessness is not always punishment; most frequently, it is God's silence: "Therefore God *gave them up* in the lusts of their hearts to impurity. . . . God *gave them up* to degrading passions. . . . God *gave them up* to a debased mind" (Rom 1:24–28; emphasis added). In godlessness, there is inherent godforsakenness; in sin, there is inherent punishment.

In his suffering in Gethsemane and his death on the cross at Golgotha, Jesus Christ went through the utter misery of being forsaken by God so that he might be nearer to us in our godlessness and godforsakenness as the "Son of God," who, as our brother, makes us children of God. This is the *divine solidarity* that manifests itself in the Passion of Christ. It is also called the "love of God": "If God is for us, who is against us? He who did not withhold his own Son, but *gave him up* for all of us, will he not with him also give us everything else?" (Rom 8:31–32).

Notice the repetition of the word in the Greek—*paradidonai*—which means "to give up" or "to sacrifice": Christ was forsaken by God in order that he might be nearer the godforsaken. God is *with* us, the godless, and he is *for* us, the godforsaken. This is the divine redemption from evil. Isaiah 53 proclaims this "for us" in describing the anguish Christ suffered in our stead: "Surely he has borne our infirmities and carried our diseases. . . . But he was wounded for our transgressions, crushed for our iniquities; upon him was the punishment that made us whole, and by his bruises we are healed" (Isa 53:4–5). In the history of theology, Christ's suffering has often been interpreted as the punishment for misdeeds: "He has fully paid for all my sins with his precious blood, and has set me free from the tyranny of the devil" (Heidelberg Catechism, question 1). These are images that are meant to explain the unfathomable "for us" of God's love as expressed in Christ's passion and death. But God is not a debt collector intent on collecting what is owed. Such images cannot account for the personal and universal mortal sin of godlessness: I do not *have* sins, I *am* a sinner. Such images miss the very foundation of mortal existence: desolation. And they likewise ignore God's very core: love. With their legal sense of guilt, they neglect the creative justice of a God who "justifies the ungodly" (Rom 4:5). They fail to account for the fact that God is concerned not only with "forgiveness of sin" but also with rebirth and the renewal of creation: "Where sin increased, grace abounded all the more" (Rom 5:20). Grace does more than counter blame, for in it a new life begins.

8. JESUS'S LIFE IN LIGHT OF THE RESURRECTION

In light of the resurrection, Jesus's life story is told not as a historical biography of a dead prophet from Nazareth but rather as a living story of Christ, the Messiah. His death gives us access to his life, and his resurrection from the dead makes his life and his message of the kingdom of God eternal: "Jesus lives." The synoptic gospels are no "story of the passion with a biographical introduction" but rather the story of Jesus Christ's life with a divine future. Jesus's divine story begins when John the Baptist baptized him in the Jordan—"You are my Son, the Beloved; with you I am well pleased" (Mark 1:11)—and ends with his resurrection (Rom 1:4). His resurrection from the dead into the force of the Holy Spirit ratified, so to speak, his baptism as a son of God. That is the personal side.

His resurrection, however, also validates his message of the kingdom of God: "The time is fulfilled, and the kingdom of God has come near; repent, and believe in the good news" (Mark 1:15). Luke proclaims the gospel from the imminent kingdom of God: "The Spirit of the Lord is upon me . . . to bring good news to the poor. He has sent me to proclaim release to the captives and recovery of sight to the blind, to let the oppressed go free, to proclaim the year of the Lord's favor. Today this scripture has been fulfilled in your hearing" (4:18–21).

In Jesus's presence, the kingdom of God is "drawn near." This nearness is based on an understanding of whence this kingdom comes: we pray that the kingdom should come "on earth as it is in heaven." Thus it comes neither from a chronological point in the future nor from a geographical point from Jerusalem; it comes from another, divine world into our human, earthly world.

The kingdom of God is the salvation of the earth and of the earthly community of all living beings. The *resurrection* is the beginning of God's new world. In this respect, both images of the future belong together. The resurrection of the dead occurs in the "life of the coming world of God." The kingdom of God means life for the poor, the ill, the blind, the oppressed. The miracles Jesus worked—related in the Gospels—are miracles of the kingdom of God and life from everlasting life. This is why such miracles accompany the course of the good news proclaiming the imminent kingdom of God.

Jesus's entire life, from his birth until his death, was resurrected. The "Christ child" is just as present as the preacher delivering the Sermon on the Mount; he who called the disciples is just as present as the "Man of Sorrows" on the Romans' cross. Eternity in a temporal sense implicitly means simultaneity.

9. IN THE REIGN OF JESUS CHRIST

Jesus's resurrection from the dead also represents his appointment as *Lord* over the kingdom of God, over the world, over heaven and earth and all that exists. Christ's dominion is universal: in his letter to the Philippians, Paul cites an early Christian confession when he writes, "Every tongue should confess that Jesus Christ is Lord, to the glory of God the Father" (2:11).

Believers live within Christ's dominion, which is why Paul speaks of "our Lord."

The title "Lord" comes from Israel. The ancient Jewish confession of faith, the Shema Yisrael, recognizes the "Lord, our God." Yahweh—Adonai—this is not just some dominion of some gods but rather a word that represents freedom.

In the words of the first commandment, "I am the Lord your God, who brought you out of the land of Egypt, out of the house of slavery" (Exod 20:2).

The "Lord" is the God of Exodus. At the same time, it is the Shekhinah of Israel's God—the compassionate presence of the Divine—that accompanies Israel: "I have observed the misery of my people who are in Egypt; I have heard their cry on account of their taskmasters. Indeed, I know their sufferings, and I have come down to deliver them" (Exod 3:7–8).

Martin Luther recognized in Jesus the Lord of Israel:

Ask who this may be:
Lord of hosts is he!
Christ Jesus our Lord,
God's only Son, adored.

(ELW 503)

When we profess our faith in "Jesus, the Lord," we think thus of the God of Israel in Exodus—"Where the Spirit of the

Lord is, there is freedom" (2 Cor 3:17)—and of God descending to take up residence in Israel, in Shekhinah, rather than of political dominion or masculine dominance. The Lord, "our God," is entirely different from the lords of this world.

Believers do not live *under* Christ's dominion like slaves but rather *in* Christ's dominion as sisters and brothers of their "first-born" brother, Jesus (Rom 8:29). The "dominion" of Christ is the "great expanse" of freedom and the sense of security in which mortal life can develop and flourish. Even on our deathbeds, there is comfort in the fellowship of Christ, for the Resurrected is present even in death. Christ goes with the dying through the night of death into the eternal light. He is standing, so to speak, on the opposite shore to receive us.

Paul outlines this life and death in the fellowship of Christ in this oft-cited passage: "We do not live to ourselves, and we do not die to ourselves. If we live, we live to the Lord, and if we die, we die to the Lord; so then, whether we live or whether we die, we are the Lord's. For to this end Christ died and lived again, so that he might be Lord of both the dead and the living" (Rom 14:7–9).

There is something that connects life and death: the dominion of Christ—that is, believers' fellowship in Christ. If we do not live only for ourselves, then neither do we die only for ourselves. This arouses fear in life and even more so in death. If we live in faith, then we do not live in ourselves but rather in the fellowship of Christ. Paul can say, "It is no longer I who live, but it is Christ who lives in me" (Gal 2:20). Are the dead for whom Christ died still dead in Christ's dominion, or have they already come back to life with Him, the Resurrected One? Since Paul mentions "the living" after "the dead," I assume that "the dead" over whom he is Lord are restored to life with his return to life.

While imprisoned, Paul wrote to the congregation in Philippi: "For to me, living is Christ and dying is gain . . . my desire is to depart and be with Christ" (1:21–23). He expects to be awakened immediately into Christ's presence.

The letter to the Ephesians, presumably written by a pupil of Paul's, continues in this vein: "[God] raised us up with

[Christ] and seated us with him in the heavenly places in Christ Jesus" (2:6). He quotes, "Sleeper, awake! Rise from the dead, and Christ will shine on you" (5:14). One might interpret this thus: because you will be resurrected with Christ, wake up here and now, see the light, and "live as children of light" (5:8).

10. HISTORICAL EVIDENCE OF JESUS'S RESURRECTION?

Was there an "empty tomb"? It is hardly conceivable that the apostles would have heard that the tomb was empty and then considered for themselves how it had come to be so and devised the idea of "resurrection by God" themselves. More likely is that the apparitions of the "living" Jesus were the reason for their Easter faith. But why didn't they have the idea that he had been taken directly into heaven? Presumably because they did have to account for the empty tomb. These two experiences together suggested the interpretation of his having undergone a "resurrection from the dead."

A historical clue: forty days after their having run away from the powerless death of their "master" on the Romans' cross, the apostles are once again in the streets of Jerusalem. They had initially gone to Galilee, fleeing from the Roman authorities. They had sought safety in their homeland. And now they are back in Jerusalem? Any other place would have been safer for them. Jesus had been executed by the Roman occupation as a "terrorist" against the Roman Empire. As associates of this "terrorist," they had to fear persecution, imprisonment, and even death. How was their fear transformed into religious courage? The only answer that makes sense to me is that they were convinced of Jesus's resurrection and their own resurrection with him.

The miracle of Pentecost occurred in Jerusalem fifty days after their having taken flight. They were "filled with the Holy Spirit"—the divine Spirit of Life took hold of them—and Peter delivered his pentecostal sermon on the resurrection of Jesus Christ: "But God raised him up, having freed him from death, because it was impossible for him to be held in its power" (Acts 2:24). He went on to cite Psalm 16:8–11.

Jesus's tomb was empty. Otherwise, the disciples would have looked ridiculous in Jerusalem with their message of resurrection, for anyone could have checked the tomb. There is furthermore no historical evidence for the contemporary reports that the disciples conspired to make Jesus's corpse disappear. Proclaiming the resurrection of a "terrorist" would have been too dangerous, given the power of the Roman occupation.

The disciples proclaimed the corporal resurrection of Jesus from his tomb: Jesus's body—which had been killed, buried, and preserved—was raised from the dead by God, his Father, through the vitality of the Holy Spirit. We want to see what this means for our life and our death and our experience of watching those we love die.

3

Our Resurrection in
the Hour of Our Death

Paul refers to Christ as having been "raised from the dead, the first fruits of those who have died" (1 Cor 15:20), but there is a distinction to be made between Christ's resurrection and our own—namely, that the body of Jesus was resurrected from his tomb. His corpse was "unspoiled" after three days, which the apostles interpreted as the fulfillment of a prophecy from the Old Testament (Acts 2:27). He "appeared" in the flesh to the women and the apostles, his physical being reanimated by the Spirit of the resurrection and transfigured by divine majesty, though the apostles could identify the scars that had been inflicted on that being in death. Our resurrection is different in this respect.

1. WE ARE NOT RESURRECTED FROM OUR GRAVES BUT IN OUR HOUR OF DEATH

Unlike Jesus, our corpse decays quickly, or our ashes are scattered over the earth. It is not our corpse that is raised from the grave but the entirety of our lived life that is resurrected in the hour of death to eternal life. In the words of the traditional funeral liturgy,

From dust thou art taken;
to dust thou shalt return;
and from the dust shalt thou rise again
at the last day.[1]

This means on the "last day" of the world's time when time ends and eternity begins. This "last day" is based on the chronicles of the world. The "last day" is also called the "Day of Days."

But what is my, and your, "last day"? When does your, does my, life end? The answer must be in the hour of death. This is why we may anticipate our resurrection in the hour of death. When we bury or cremate a corpse, we can rest assured that the soul of the deceased has already been resurrected and awakened. And so, we add, at the grave's edge, "Jesus Christ, our Savior, has resurrected you. Praise and thanks be to God. You have reached eternal life."

When Dietrich Bonhoeffer was taken from his cell at the Flossenbürg concentration camp on April 9, 1945, to be led to his execution, he took leave of his fellow prisoners with the following words: "This is the end—for me, the beginning of life."

Our hour of death is the hour of our resurrection. When we die, we wake to eternal life. The pains of death are the birth pains into eternal life. While our body with the "sum" of its limbs lies dead and decays, the entirety of our life, the "whole" of our living soul, will rise again with a new body to everlasting life. The new body in the resurrection—the *soma pneumatikon*—will be a body intensely alive in the divine life force in accordance with the body of the resurrected Christ, which was "transfigured" in the majesty of God. It will take that form that God saw fit for us in the world to come. An oft-cited poem by Hermann Hesse can be interpreted not only from a Buddhist perspective but also in terms of Christian conviction:

1   Charles Augustus Goodrich, *The Universal Traveller: Designed to Introduce Readers at Home to an Acquaintance with the Arts, Customs, and Manners of the Principal Modern Nations on the Globe*, 4th ed. (New York: Collins, Sheldon, and Converse, 1838), 92.

Maybe death's hour too will send us out
new-born towards undreamed-of lands, maybe
life's call to us will never find an end . . .
Courage my heart, take leave and fare thee well![2]

2. THE "NEW BODY" IN THE RESURRECTION ACCORDING TO PAUL

Anyone who hears of the resurrection soon asks the same question Paul asked: "How are the dead raised? With what kind of body do they come?" (1 Cor 15:35). Apparently, Paul cannot fathom a continued existence after death without a physical body as, for example, suggested in the doctrine of the immortality of an incorporeal soul. Paul tells those "fools" who would pose such questions to consider death and becoming in nature: "What you sow does not come to life unless it dies" (1 Cor 15:36).

It is just a single grain that is sown, a seed placed in the soil, from which comes a beautiful flower or a mighty tree. The grain of wheat ceases being a grain; Paul imagines that it "dies," only to take on a new form and grow into a stalk of wheat. On fruitful soil, it does not perish. He applies this analogy to the death of the natural body and the resurrection of the body to eternal life:

So it is with the resurrection of the dead.
What is sown is perishable, what is raised is imperishable.
It is sown in dishonor, it is raised in glory.
It is sown in weakness, it is raised in power.
It is sown a physical body, it is raised a spiritual body.

(1 Cor 15:42–44)

While the fragile mortal body tends toward decay, degeneracy, and inadequacy, it contains within it a life that, if only

---

2   Hermann Hesse, *Magister Ludi*, trans. Mervyn Savill (London: Aldus, 1949), 396. Cited in Joseph Campbell, *The Mysteries* (Princeton, NJ: Princeton University Press, 1978), 118.

sown and not withheld, germinates into the eternal life of immortality, glory, and strength.

I understand this analogy of sowing to mean that life must be lived, life must be employed for the sake of the future: "If you won't stake your life anon, Ne'er will a life for you be won!"[3] So much of life is left unlived—unloved and neglected. The Christian life is one of love and hope, a life of sowing and sacrifice. The fruitful soil of the earth has been drenched with so much blood shed at the hands of warring clans and murderous humans. The seeds for the kingdom of God on earth are service in the name of peace and the fight for justice, love of one's neighbor and one's enemy, cessation of armed conflict, and healing.

Is the body of the resurrection a new body of eternal life or a transfigured body of this mortal life? The *entire life* is resurrected, healed, and transfigured. The entirety of life is shaped by its form (*Gestalt*) and its course: "God gives it a body as he has chosen, and to each kind of seed its own body" (1 Cor 15:38). Paul's expectations include the animals—both wild and domestic—the fish, the earth, the sun, the moon, and stars in the heavens. Because each reflects the joy of the creature, each has its own sheen or glory—the Greek word Paul uses here, *doxa*, can also mean "beauty" or "splendor."

What do the inhuman elements of creation have to do with resurrection? We consider what Paul wrote to the Romans (8:19–39) about how "creation waits with eager longing" to be freed from its "bondage to decay": "Creation was subjected to futility . . . [yet] in hope. . . . We know that the whole creation has been groaning in labor pains until now" (Rom 8:20–22).

Is this futile, temporary creation the seed for a new, everlasting creation? The futility of this creation would thus culminate in "death," which leads in turn to resurrection and the everlasting life. The natural cycle of "death and birth" is

---

3   Friedrich Schiller, *Wallenstein's Camp*, trans. Theodor Wirgman (London: David Nutt, 1871), 103.

ultimately resolved not in favor of death and universal demise but rather in favor of birth and life.

Paul calls that which we call "fleeting" the "perishable"—or "rot-able." Everything that lives and dies is perishable. Jesus's corpse, however, did not rot before it was resurrected. Paul states two convictions regarding the future of the perishable:

1. Nor does the perishable inherit the imperishable (1 Cor 15:50).
2. For this perishable body must put on imperishability (1 Cor 15:53).

There is no continuity from here to there, but there is continuity from there to here. How does this happen?

Death has been swallowed up in victory—life conquers! (1 Cor 15:54)

He will swallow up death forever. (Isa 25:8)

When Paul uses the natural cycle of "death and birth" as an analogy to describe the death and reawakening of a mortal life, he simultaneously widens the mortal future to include the future of all that is perishable, which is to say, to include the future of everything that lives. This incorporates the future of humankind into a "planetary solidarity" with all that lives. In a similar vein, he explains the solidarity of our "groans" and "longing" for the liberation of the body with the "groans and longing" of "all creation" in his letter to the Romans (8:22–23). The eternal life in God's new creation takes shape. The new earth will begin with the rousing and awakening of all that lives and will be enriched and beautified with the rousing and awakening of humankind. Everything created by God will be brought back and resurrected. Nothing will be lost. Everything will be completed.

3. PAUL'S "MYSTERY"

> Listen, I will tell you a mystery! We will not all die, but we will
> all be changed. (1 Cor 15:51)

Paul expected the end of this world's era within his own life-
time. In typically apocalyptic terms, he described the end: "In
a moment, in the twinkling of an eye, at the last trumpet. For
the trumpet will sound, and the dead will be raised imperishable, and we will be changed" (1 Cor 15:52).

He was mistaken. Only a few years after writing these lines,
he was executed in Rome—unchanged and yet already resurrected! The end of this manifestation of the world did not come
during his lifetime. He expressed the imminence of the end in
temporal terms: "The appointed time has grown short" (1 Cor
7:29). This "shortness" of time is not, however, to be measured
in seconds but rather a question of the density of time under
the pressure of that which happens within it. We experience the
same quantity of time as "long" or "short" depending on what
we experience during that period. Paul was familiar with this
sense of experienced time, for how could he expect the sud-
denness of the world's end "in a moment, in the twinkling of an
eye"? He certainly would not have been very concerned with
his apocalyptic speculations, for the future era is fulfilled in
the preparatory apocalyptic act of Jesus Christ having been
resurrected *from the dead*: "Death has been swallowed up
in victory. . . . But thanks be to God, who gives us the victory
through our Lord Jesus Christ" (1 Cor 15:54–57).

Those who read Paul's predictions about the end of this
world could answer by citing another passage from his letter
to the Romans: "If we live, we live to the Lord, and if we die, we
die to the Lord" (Rom 14:8). Viewing the future in light of the
resurrection of Jesus Christ lends one calm and reassurance in
the face of alarmist, apocalyptic proclamations, then and now.

Christoph Friedrich Blumhardt is supposed to have com-
forted a dying man afraid of "the long night of death" with

the following words: "Don't you worry about that: it is only a moment until the resurrection."

4. DOES SOMETHING ELSE OCCUR BETWEEN DEATH AND REAWAKENING? THE QUESTION OF AN "IN-BETWEEN STATE"

Just as the "last day" commences in the hour of death, so too does one come before the "last judgment." The "singular judgment" is the individual anticipation of the "Great Judgment" of the world. After death, mortals are confronted with the true entirety of their lives and appointed their own judge. Those who believe in Christ have been forgiven for their sins, but the individual has yet to do penance for the consequences of those sins. The goal is the perfection of the individual in accordance with God's ordainment. The Catholic tradition speaks in this context of purgatory.

In the second part of his *Divine Comedy*, Dante describes purgatory as a mountain of purification where individuals are spiritually cleansed and ascend toward the heavens: "Let us go toward them, for they slowly come, thou, sweet son, be steadfast in thy hope" (canto III).[4] In apocalyptic visions, heaven and hell are seen as end stations, but in purgatory, God's story with humankind continues after death. The Reformers Luther and Calvin rejected "purgatory" because it had led in Catholic doctrine to the peddling of so-called indulgences, but if one considers the shortcomings and lapses of life, it becomes clear that something must come between death and resurrection.

So much in our lives remains unfinished: We begin things without seeing them through. We have failed. We have remained silent where we should have spoken. We have failed to speak the truth because we were afraid, and our faith wavered. How

4   Dante Alighieri, *The Divine Comedy of Dante Alighieri*, trans. Courtney Langdon, vol. 2 (Cambridge, MA: Harvard University Press, 1920), 31.

can a life here ever be "completed" and truly closed? But what God begins, he also brings to completion (Phil 1:6).

It is thoughts like these that lead us to consider how the course of our story with God continues after our death. Jörg Zink put it this way:

> I think, according to what the gospel suggests, that I will have to re-suffer much and re-live much, will have to bemourn much that was neglected; but that I shall not perish of it all, because God's goodness will hold me fast. I think that I shall have to suffer a transformation into the one I was really destined to be, until . . . harmony with the nature and will of God is finally attained, and the forgiveness takes place which must be pronounced before existence can achieve the fullness and power for which it was really intended. Until that Figure, that great counterpart God, says: it's all right—everything is all right. Now come and fill the place and take up the tasks intended for you, for the great future of my kingdom.[5]

I agree completely with this explanation of what happens between death and eternal life in the kingdom of God. I will only add:

Consider, as well, the life of those who were not allowed or able to live. Consider the lives cut short or destroyed: how are they "finished"? The beloved child who died at birth; the four-year-old boy who was run over by a car; the handicapped brother who never consciously lived; the friend, just sixteen years old, obliterated by a bomb right next to you that leaves you unscathed . . .

To imagine that it was "all over" when they died would cast the entire world into absurdity. For if their lives had no purpose, do ours have any? It is the conviction that God's story continues with such lives even after death, with lives

---

5   Jörg Zink, *Erinnerungen: Sieh nach den Sternen—gib acht auf die Gassen*, 2nd ed. (Stuttgart: Kreuz, 1992), 393. English translation cited from Jürgen Moltmann, *The Coming of God: Christian Eschatology*, trans. Margaret Kohl (Minneapolis: Fortress, 2005), 117.

that have been prematurely ended and destroyed, that allows us to embrace and cherish life in this world despite the various handicaps, disease, and violence that interfere with life around us. I think that the Spirit that brings everlasting life also offers further space in which life that has been crippled or destroyed can move freely. Just as Jesus healed the sick on earth, the Resurrected Christ will heal those diseases that afflicted and hindered life here. The life destroyed by violence will be lifted up and lived in full. And so I think that eternal life will grant the downtrodden, the handicapped, and the ruined the space and time and power to live life as it was intended for them and for which they were born. This is in accordance with God's righteousness, which, I believe, is the very essence and passion of the Divine.

5. MARTIN LUTHER'S LOGIC

Luther conceived of the dead in a state of deep sleep that transcends time and space, without consciousness or sensation. When Christ wakes the dead on the "last day," he thought, they will know neither where they were nor how long they have been dead. In other words, "as soon as thy eyes have closed shalt thou be woken."[6]

This image of death as "sleep" is no mere euphemism for death but a way to express the hope that there is something else to come—namely, the resurrection and eternal life—just as we go to sleep in the evening only to wake the next morning. The hour of death is the hour of resurrection. Luther developed a concept of time and eternity to explain this: "Now since before God there is no reckoning of time, before Him a thousand years must be as one day. Therefore Adam, the first man, is just as close to Him as the man who will be born last before the Last Day. For God does not see time longitudinally; He sees it transversely, as if you were looking transversely at

6   Cited from Jürgen Moltmann, *In the End—the Beginning: The Life of Hope*, trans. Margaret Kohl (Minneapolis: Fortress, 2004), 111.

a tall tree lying before you. . . . Then you can see both ends at the same time."[7]

Eternity is not to be understood as outside of time but as containing all of time simultaneously. When we think in terms of going from here to there, the mortal hours of death are strung out over time. We are thinking in terms of a linear chronology: individuals are born, live, die, and decay. This has been the case since the beginning of humankind and will continue as long as humans exist. If, however, we think in terms of "from there to here," all the mortal hours of death fall on the resurrection day. The storm winds of the resurrection sweep the last and first human being up to resurrection from death within a single moment! Hanging on the cross, Christ says to the man crucified next to him *today*—not in three days, not on the last day—"Truly I tell you, today you will be with me in Paradise" (Luke 23:43).

Catholic theologians like Karl Rahner, Gisbert Greshake, and others have conducted a similar thought experiment in order to argue for a "resurrection in death" (i.e., at the moment of death). This, however, would make indulgences for the deceased in purgatory and masses said for their benefit entirely superfluous. Joseph Ratzinger thus formally dismissed such a doctrine in the name of the Roman Catholic Church as soon as he became prefect of the Congregation for the Doctrine of the Faith.[8] The decree issued reads, "The Church affirms that a spiritual element survives and subsists after death, an element endowed with consciousness and will, so

---

7   Martin Luther, "Sermons on the Second Epistle of St. Peter," in *The Catholic Epistles*, ed. Jaroslav Pelikan and Walter A. Hansen, trans. Martin H. Bertram, Luther's Works 30 (St. Louis: Concordia, 2007), 196.

8   Editor's Note: While Ratzinger's *Eschatology* (published in German in 1977) addresses many of the same themes, the CDF letter here quoted was written by Franjo Cardinal Seper two years prior to Ratzinger's appointment as prefect of the Congregation for the Doctrine of the Faith.

that the 'human self' subsists (although admittedly losing its corporeality entirely in this interim period)."[9]

Ratzinger's thesis is untenable if one considers individuals who experience brain death. Or should the soul in this interim period possess a certain brain? In which case, it would hardly be possible to justify burial. Or might electronic "brains" be able to bridge this "in-between period"?

The shortcoming of the theological discussion over this "interim state" lies in the fact that it has usually begun with the "human self" of mankind or with the eternity of God rather than with Christ's resurrection. In the latter case, the commemoration of the dead is not rendered superfluous.

6. THE FELLOWSHIP OF CHRIST IN LIFE, DEATH, AND RESURRECTION

Jesus was not only awakened as the "first" but also to preside as "Lord" over God's dominion. God intends the authority of Jesus Christ to be universal. Paul cites a hymn to Christ: "So that at the name of Jesus every knee should bend, in heaven and on earth and under the earth, and every tongue should confess that Jesus Christ is Lord, to the glory of God the Father" (Phil 2:10–11).

For believers, the dominion of Jesus Christ represents the fellowship of Christ. It is in the universal space of Christ's dominion that fellowship in Christ develops. Faith is more than trusting in God; it leads the believer into fellowship with Jesus in life and in death. Living with Jesus means experiencing

9   Translator's Note: As is the Vatican's custom, this decree was issued in multiple languages, including English and German. The first sentence cited here is quoted directly from Franjo Cardinal Seper, "Letter on Certain Questions Concerning Eschatology" (Sacred Congregation for the Doctrine of the Faith, May 17, 1979), http://www.vatican.va/roman_curia/congregations/cfaith/documents/rc_con_cfaith_doc_19790517_escatologia_en.html. The second clause in the sentence Moltmann cites from the German version of the decree, however ("wobei es freilich in der Zwischenzeit seiner vollen Körperlichkeit entbehrt"), has no clear counterpart in the Vatican's English translation. I have thus provided my own translation of this clause, placed here in parentheses.

healing and comfort in Christian discipleship and adhering to the Sermon on the Mount. Dying in fellowship with Christ is dying with hope. Being resurrected with Christ means entering into divine joy. Fellowship in Christ grants life in the divine love that Jesus embodies: "For I am convinced that neither death, nor life, nor angels, nor rulers, nor things present, nor things to come, nor powers . . . will be able to separate us from the love of God in Christ Jesus our Lord" (Rom 8:38–39).

It is this conviction that allows us to entrust ourselves and this endangered world to the Lord Jesus Christ rather than continuing to consider worriedly what the future may hold: "Whether we live or whether we die, we are the Lord's" (Rom 14:8). We can die in this certainty, trusting that in the hereafter of which we know nothing, Christ will resurrect us to enter into the kingdom of God: "For to this end Christ died and lived again, so that he might be Lord of both the dead and the living" (Rom 14:9).

Paul's Epistle to the Ephesians places even more emphasis on this fellowship in Christ: "But God . . . out of the great love with which he loved us . . . made us alive together with Christ . . . and raised us up with him" (2:4–6).

Isaiah 60:1—"Arise, shine; for your light has come"—is incorporated into the Christian wake-up call: "Sleeper, awake! Rise from the dead, and Christ will shine on you" (Eph 5:14).

The natural certainty of death is outshone by faith's certainty of the resurrection. As we lay dying, we can see through the night falling around us to the eternal light of God's glory, and we will greet every "new" day in this life in the light of Christ's day.

A life in fellowship with the resurrected Christ is eternal life here and now, for fellowship with Christ in faith represents a close tie to him. Paul and John expressed it this way: I am *in* Christ—and Christ is *in* me. This means my little life is contained within his divine life, and his resurrected life works in my mortal life: "Your life is hidden with Christ in God" (Col 3:3); "It is no longer I who live, but it is Christ who lives in me" (Gal 2:20).

Life in fellowship with Christ is not an end station; Christ's dominion has a future: "For you have died, and your life is hidden with Christ in God. When Christ who is your life is revealed, then you also will be revealed with him in glory" (Col 3:3–4).

The kingdom of the glory of God is the future of Christ's dominion and the future of the believer's fellowship in Christ.

When we die, we awake in a hopeful place in eternal life that is illuminated by that "bright and morning star, Light of light without beginning." This dawn is not yet as bright as full daylight. The beginning is not the fulfillment but rather a divine promise of fulfillment. The awakening is the first step toward resurrection into eternal life.

In my book *The Coming of God: Christian Eschatology* (first published in 1995 and in English in 1996), I accordingly interpreted Christ's reign as "the promise of the kingdom of God."[10] At the time, I accepted Ernst Käsemann's concept of "eschatological reservation" rather than transforming this negative idea into a positive concept of "eschatological anticipation." It is not a question of what is *not yet* present within Christ's dominion but rather a question of eternal life, which is *already* present within the fellowship of Christ. I understood it to mean "the dead are dead and not yet risen, but they are already 'in Christ' and are with him on the way to his future. When he appears in glory, they will be beside him and will live eternally with him."[11] That which I understood then as a "promise" applying to the future I see today as a "real beginning."

In 1995, I rejected a "resurrection in death," for it appeared too individualistic to me. Now my perspective has changed, and I accept this position. Instead of looking from the present into the future that has yet to pass, I look from the future to the beginning of the present. Our resurrection into eternal life is inherent in our fellowship with Christ. The glory of God illuminates the life hidden in Christ as its future.

---

10   Moltmann, *The Coming of God*, 104ff.

11   Moltmann, *The Coming of God*, 105.

While the Christian fellowship of believers is exclusive, the dominion of Christ is universal. The Spirit of the resurrection blows from the resurrected Christ throughout all of the history of mankind and the cosmos. In this life before death, the Spirit that grants life serves as a life force, and there, in death, it brings each life to its intended fullness. If the deceased have already been reawakened in eternal life, then we are separated from them by time, but they are within eternity with us. They are waiting for us and, I think, watching over us.

4

The Death and Resurrection of a Living Soul

In 1997, my wife, Elisabeth, titled her autobiography "Whoever does not touch the earth cannot reach heaven."[1] She closed the book with the following words: "It was as if I had touched the earth and the earth touched me. And it was still amazing, and I was still curious at the way in which heaven opened above."[2]

What she meant with this "touching the earth" is manifest in her writing. She wrote nothing more about "reaching heaven."

1. THE DUAL WORLD: HEAVEN AND EARTH

The Bible portrays creation as a dualistic world of heaven and earth, and Genesis goes into much more detail about the formation of the earth than about that of heaven. It is worth noting that there is *one* earth but *many* heavens—according to the popular poetic notion, there are seven. The ancient church

---

1   Translator's Note: Elisabeth Moltmann-Wendel's autobiography was published in English under the title *Autobiography*. The phrase here is a translation of the German title of her autobiography.

2   Elisabeth Moltmann-Wendel, *Autobiography*, trans. John Bowden (London: SCM Press, 1997), 174.

in the Greco-Roman tradition and the Nicene Creed spoke of the "visible and invisible" world—or, in some translations, of all that is "seen and unseen." Between these visible and invisible worlds, there is no spatial distance as between heaven and earth; both are equally close to mankind.

Small children learn to pray to God:

Take me when I die to heaven
happy there with thee to dwell.

God is in heaven, and heaven is there where God's love flows. "Heaven" is thus symbolically linked with the security (*Geborgenheit*) and blessedness (*Seligkeit*) that comes from God. The deceased are "in heaven." What do we imagine that to mean? There is an old tradition of opening a window at the hour of death so that the soul of the deceased can ascend to heaven:

Whereat my soul extended
its wings towards skies to roam:
O'er quiet lands, suspended,
my soul was flying home.[3]

When the deceased are "in heaven," they are within the "invisible" world. They are in a sort of "second present" with their entire life stories and their conscious souls. We can remember their stories and rest assured that they are there even as we go on living. We can consciously live with them. In Asian cultures, the ancestors are not considered dead. The descendants live together with their ancestors. The Christian hope of resurrection leads us not to look back to our "ancient forebears" as the point of unification but rather to look into the future unification in the kingdom of God.

3   Josef Karl Benedikt von Eichendorff, "Moonlit Night," trans. Walter A. Aue (2008), LiederNet Archive, https://www.lieder.net/lieder/get_text.html?TextId=38193.

The more the earth is experienced and suffered as a "vale of tears," the more we expect heaven to be a "homeland" or "haven" for the soul. When does heaven touch the earth? In the spring—

> It was like Heaven's glimmer
> caressed the Earth within
> that in Her blossom's shimmer
> She had to think of Him.[4]

In poetic terms, the "heavens"[5] (*Himmel*) frequently correspond to the state of the earth below. Gray clouds hang over it in a foreboding fashion; Shakespeare sets the somber mood for his play *Henry VI* with the opening line, "Hung be the heavens with black." The German author Christa Wolf's novel *Divided Heaven* alludes in the title to the division of the two Germanies, and the German filmmaker Wim Wender's film *Der Himmel über Berlin* (lit. "Heaven over Berlin," marketed in English under the title *Wings of Desire*) highlights the unity of one sky over the divided city. In the Bible, the heavens "were opened" when Jesus was baptized in the Jordan (Matt 3:16), and the resurrected Christ ascended into the heavens as the clouds parted to receive him. The apostle Stephen, shortly before he was stoned to death, proclaimed, "I see the heavens opened and the Son of Man standing at the right hand of God!" (Acts 7:56).

In the Our Father, we pray that the first three petitions might come to pass "on earth as it is in heaven." In heaven, the name of God is hallowed, God's kingdom has arrived, and God's will is done. Heaven is the world in alignment with God, the counterpart to this blood-drenched earth. When we pray "on earth as it is in heaven," we draw that world in alignment with God down to this contradictory earth, so that this earth

---

4   Eichendorff, "Moonlit Night."

5   Translator's Note: German uses the same word, *Himmel*, for both "heaven" and "sky."

can become a soundboard that resonates with heaven. The believer who prays the Our Father wants to have "heaven on earth" despite all the contradictions. The "kingdom of God" should come to earth as it is in heaven. "Touching the earth" and "reaching heaven" thus go hand in hand. Whoever truly touches the earth reaches heaven, and whoever reaches heaven touches the earth. In the kingdom of God, heaven and earth permeate each other. In the joy of God, the earth touches us even as the heavens open for us. Heaven becomes earthly and the earth becomes "heavenly." Heaven is no longer "above" and the earth is no longer "below," but rather heaven and earth together surround us completely. In the words of Psalm 139, God "hems" us in, he is "behind and before" us.

2. THE DUAL WORLD: THIS LIFE AND THE BEYOND

In the *Theology of Hope* (German edition 1964, English translation 1967) and my wife's feminist theology, we were persuaded by Dietrich Bonhoeffer's letters from prison—which were published in 1951 and fascinated us during our studies in Göttingen—that there is a "profound this-worldliness" inherent in Christianity. In Bonhoeffer's eyes, this Christian "this-worldliness" was "profound" because it was characterized by "the constant knowledge of death and resurrection."[6] This differentiates it from the banal "this-worldliness" of nonbelievers.

Now, however, we want to appraise the profound "other-worldliness" of the Christian faith, which is constantly aware of God's incarnation and of Jesus Christ's death. This differentiates it from the Gnostic redemptive religions.

Nonbelievers live entirely in this world and forgo the hereafter. This is *naturalism*, which uses the laws of nature to explain all that is and accepts natural death as a fact of life. What

---

6 John W. de Gruchy, ed., *The Cambridge Companion to Dietrich Bonhoeffer* (Cambridge: Cambridge University Press, 1999), 240.

is, however, a "natural death"? Without a hereafter, there is no world here and now.

The Gnostic religion of redemption did in fact refer to this world as "strange" and characterize life in this world as one of "alienation" in which souls—divine sparks of light—achieve redemption in their true homeland of the hereafter. The true homeland of the soul is thereby that heaven—the hereafter—from which it springs. There is, however, no longing for redemption absent an affirmation of life in this world with its joys and burdens. One exists only with the other: this world and the world to come, immanence and transcendence. When one takes seriously the death and resurrection of Christ and God's incarnation, one becomes incarnate oneself.

In the experience of death—be it that of one we hold dear or our own—we become conscious of a profound discontinuity between this world and the hereafter. There is no path from this world over the frontier into the hereafter, but perhaps there is a path from the hereafter to this world. Is death the total eradication of life? Or is there a continuity of the soul that dies and is awakened to eternal life? In many cultures, death is considered to be the step in this world that leads to rebirth in the hereafter. In birth, the sheltered life of an infant in the mother's womb ends and a life in the "hereafter" begins in which the baby encounters this world of the senses by breathing and nursing. Does this process of birth work as a metaphor for the process of dying? If so, death is our birth into everlasting life.

3. THE DIALECTIC OF SACRIFICE AND RESURRECTION

The "profound this-worldliness" and the extreme "other-worldliness" of Christian faith can also be understood as a dialectic of sacrifice and resurrection. Paul and John both used the analogy of a seed and plant. When the seed falls on the earth, it "dies," but, as Paul says, it "transforms itself" into the plant that flourishes. The seed carries within it the germ of the plant that is to grow, but no plant can be "resurrected" unless the seed falls to the earth and "dies." I understand the parable to mean that the deeper our love for this life is and the more unreservedly we affirm it, the more we can delight in the happiness of this life and the joys it has to offer, even though we also conversely experience the process of death—be it of a loved one or our own—more intensely.

It must be lived. Every day we are meant to open our eyes to the miracle of life, to feel and taste it, to love and dance.

This means that we experience life and death in love. It is easy enough to test this: when we no longer love anything, not even ourselves, we become apathetic and no longer care whether we live or die. I knew such people during the war. Life no longer had any meaning for them, and neither did death. The more we "throw ourselves into life's arms," the more certain we become of the resurrection and eternal life. This works the other way around as well, for the more totally we trust in resurrection and eternal life, the more we can love this life—and the lives of those dear to us—with abandon, loving all that lives and our life together here on earth. We no longer have to cling to anything, not even to ourselves. It will all be restored in the end. The more we "touch" the earth, the wider heaven opens to us.

Marie Luise Kaschnitz has a poem:

Resurrection
Sometimes we arise
Arise for the resurrection
In bright daylight
Our hair alive
Our skins breathing.[7]

Life and death are not the problems confronting mankind; rather, *love and death* are. Does love die with the death of a

7   Marie Luise Kaschnitz, "Resurrection," in *Selected Later Poems of Marie Luise Kaschnitz*, trans. Lisel Mueller (Princeton, NJ: Princeton University Press, 1980), 61.

loved one, or is love "as strong as death"? Where love is carried by hope in the resurrection and an eternal life together, it is truly stronger than death. Our mortal life has been blessed with the "seed" of the promise of everlasting life. This "seed" is love.

4. THE DUAL EXISTENCE OF BODY AND SOUL

A distinction between the "subject" and "object" of human existence can be made when an individual's consciousness expands to include reflecting on itself. In modern usage, the soul is generally not thought of in relation to the Divine but rather in its relationship to the body. The soul becomes the "self" and "owner," the body a possession to be formed and optimized. Each individual is their own invention, albeit most often the invention of the system in which they are to function.

Herein lies the difference between "being" and "having." I *am* consciously me, and I *have* a body. When I wake up in the morning, I might initially say that I do not feel well. I *am* sick. As I become more conscious, the more I am able to pinpoint the source of my discomfort, and then I say I *have* a stomachache. By changing the illness from something we *are* to something we *have*, we open the way to curing it. Nevertheless, the sick person does not disappear.

How do doctors determine whether a person is dead? In olden times, they held a mirror up to the person's mouth. If it did not cloud up, this indicated that the person was no longer breathing. It was said then that "he has breathed his last breath." From this perspective, the center of life is in the *diaphragm*. Once the circulatory system was better understood, one spoke of cardiac death, of someone's heart having stopped. When a heart ceases beating and attempts to reanimate an individual prove futile, the person is pronounced dead. This means that the center of life is in the *heart*. Today we speak of someone being "brain-dead." When the electrical impulses within the brain ebb, an individual is considered dead. This means that the center of the human being is in the *brain*. Over the course of humankind's cultural development, it could thus be said that the center of human life has risen from the diaphragm up to the brain. The modern conception of humans is primarily as "sentient beings." Everything else is their physical bodies. As modern neurological research, however, increasingly decodes the function of the brain and understands this organ as part of the body, the thinking self is no longer fixed in the body.

Modern conceptions of body and soul go back to René Descartes and the eighteenth-century physician Julien Offray de La Mettrie, who wrote the book L'homme machine (Machine Man). Descartes was of the opinion that ancient questions about God and the soul could be answered more convincingly in philosophical than theological terms, as he wrote in the dedication of his Meditations. He completed the shift in the conception of what it means to be human; instead of viewing the Platonic soul as divine substance, it was seen as an autonomous force that ruled over the mortal body. This human subject becomes conscious of itself via thought rather than through the perceptions of the senses. The body with its sensual needs and perceptions is relegated to the realm of objective things: it is "objectified." The thinking self was bound to the body—Descartes himself did not know exactly how but hypothesized it was in the pineal gland. In effect, there were two coexisting beings within each individual: a nonextended thinking thing and a nonthinking extended thing. Descartes emphasized this difference to such an extent as to state, "It is certain that I am really distinct from my body, and can exist without it."[8] Modern transhumanists are working to create artificial human brains so precisely that the thinking self could exist without a body or a brain and would thus be rendered "immortal." Descartes's follower, La Mettrie, anticipated this in his materialist book, L'homme machine, which both dissolves the psychosomatic holistic concept of humanity and abandons

8   René Descartes, Descartes: Meditations on First Philosophy: With Selections from the Objections and Replies, ed. and trans. John Cottingham, 2nd ed. (Cambridge: Cambridge University Press, 2017), 136.

an understanding of mankind's ecological position within the natural world. Humans are, Descartes wrote in his *Discourse on the Method*, "masters and possessors of nature." The soul's certainty of God is renounced in favor of the certainty of the autonomous subject in itself.

5. HOLISTIC LIFE

While the dual existence of body and soul, in the end, leads to the materialistic dissolution of human beings, I aim to understand the *soul* as an animating principle (Prinzip der Lebendigkeit). The entirety of a human life is the shape of that life (*Lebensgestalt*) in its life story. Our lives as humans are lived in social, ecological, and transcendental relationships. This is why I speak of a "living soul." Only God can grasp the entirety of a life and its story, for everything temporal is simultaneous from his perspective in eternity. This is why the transcendental point of reference is essential for us to know ourselves. In the presence of God—*coram Deo*—I am whole, despite the many fragments and contradictions of my life.

The Living Soul

The Platonic soul is divine but does not live in a mortal sense. It is immortal, for it was not born. Descartes's "thinking self" is not living in an "extended" measure. It is remarkable that the Bible and Christian hymns speak of the soul in terms of "my soul" and associate expressions of life with it. This is the living soul:

> As a deer longs for flowing streams,
> so my soul longs for you, O God.
> My soul thirsts for God,
> for the living God.

(Ps 42:1–2)

> My soul is exceedingly sorrowful, even to death.

(Mark 14:34).

Oh come my soul with singing!
With joyful sounds arise.

(German hymn by Paul Gerhardt [1653],
English translation by Miss Burlingham [1866])[9]

The mortal soul derives its "liveliness" from the "living God." Does the expression "my soul" express a relationship of possession like "my house" or "my blood"? I think it is more an expression of affinity and belonging together, along the lines of what I mean when I refer to "my family." "My soul" refers to the connections in my life that extend beyond the realm of my own consciousness. Otherwise, I could have said "I." I long for you, O God, I am exceedingly sorrowful, and I sing. I thus suggest that we should understand "the soul" as synonymous with "life": *my life* longs for you, O God; *my life* is sorrowful; *my life* sings joyfully. And with "my life," I mean "all of my life."

The extent to which "soul" means "life" can be seen in the word *animation*. Animation is often associated with "bringing to life," but its literal meaning has to do with endowing a soul. Reanimation is frequently used in the context of bringing someone back from the brink of death, but it literally means to "re-endow with a soul." Endowing someone with a soul does more than compel their body to breathe and move—it makes them lively and stimulates their love for life. It is this endowment with a soul that brings humans to life and makes life "lively." Mankind is created for a "living soul" and to delight in life.

It is difficult to recognize and control one's entire life, which is why we do well to ask in whose presence we are whole. Who has a holistic view of us? I myself am only ever conscious of part of my entire life. My memories include only fragments of my life story, and yet the rest of the story has happened.

9   English text cited from no. 423 in William Reid, *The Praise Book* (London: James Nisbet & Company, 1872). Reid does not credit a translator for the English version, but a Miss Burlingham is credited with the translation here: "Paul Gerhardt," Hymnary, accessed May 3, 2020, https://hymnary.org/person/Gerhardt_Paul.

God alone is able to survey all of a life lived. When I refer to "my soul," I refer to the part of my life oriented toward God. It is thus "a living soul" before the "living God."

It is worth noting that biblical references to the soul do not imply that it is unchangeable or stolid. Instead, the soul longs, grieves, and rejoices. (In fact, in some English translations of Psalm 42, the soul "pants," and in the traditional German rendering of this verse, it "screams" [*schreit*].) It is one with the senses; it is a corporeal soul. Is the soul's liveliness a reflection of the "living God"? Is the soul's mortal liveliness linked to "eternal life"? Is the "living soul" as unique as the "living God" of the Judeo-Christian tradition? Its liveliness is decided in death.

As the saying goes, "The whole is more than the sum of the parts." The whole is not only more than the sum of the parts but also qualitatively different. Something is said to emerge out of the whole, which has a different principle of organization and displays other qualities than the parts individually. The pieces, which together make up the parts of the whole, change their qualities. The whole cannot be explained on the basis of the parts. When this whole disappears, the parts fall apart into incoherent pieces. The whole, however, presents a possibility that can no longer be forgotten. The living soul is the wholeness of "human life."

The entirety of our life, in temporal terms, is the "story of our life." Our memory remains conscious only of fragments of it, and yet we know that it has happened. Over time, it becomes history but nevertheless *exists*. We cannot change the parts of our life story that lie in the past, but neither can we lose them.

From the perspective of our life story, the totality of our life is not a series of unconnected moments and situations; there is, rather, a continuity throughout the vicissitudes of life. It is marked with *our name*. My name is on my passport and my driver's license. With my name, I identify myself with my past and vouch for myself in the future. With my name, I acknowledge my debts and make new promises. My family name places my single life within the series of generations before and after me. My given name guarantees the continuity of my individual life story. It is an echo of faith in God's loyalty to each of us: "Do not fear, for I have redeemed you; I have called you by name, you are mine" (Isa 43:1). This divine loyalty vouches for the continuity of life, even when this continuity is hidden from us in discontinuity, as my teacher and friend, Otto Weber, believed.

The entirety of a life, in spatial terms, is the shape of a life (*Lebensgestalt*). This includes not only the shape (*Gestalt*) of our physical bodies but also the shape of the life we live. According to modern gestalt and environmental psychology, a person's life is shaped by a number of types of environments. On the one hand, there is a *natural environment*, which includes a person's genetic makeup and entire medical history. There is also a *social environment*, the society in which one grows up, as well as various social bonds that one has willingly formed or had imposed on oneself. Another factor is the *relationship to oneself*, with which an individual influences or endures the shape of one's life. In addition, there is the transcendental *divine environment* ("You hem me in, behind and before" [Ps 139:5]) in which we experience the shape of our own lives. The relationship between body and soul is only a fragmentary piece of the shape of a life. The relationship to oneself is only one relationship of many—a relationship often made too much of in our modern subjective society. In these various environments, human beings gain individuality, sociality, and a likeness to God, for the shape of their lives connects them with their environments even as it also differentiates them.

"Being whole" is also a *cry for help* that arises when the shape of a life is afflicted with turmoil. In every social relationship, I am someone else. I am like the "man without qualities" that Robert Musil describes in his novel so titled. Individuals adapt to fill the multitude of roles assigned to them in response to the wide-ranging demands made upon them. When those demands become too great or too divergent, individuals begin to lose touch with themselves. We sometimes speak of a person—or ourselves—becoming "frayed around the edges" or "unraveled." As the political upheavals of the twentieth century have shown all too well, humans are capable of considerable social and political assimilation. No life-form (*Lebensgestalt*) known to us is "whole" in the sense of "intact." Some are sitting upon the ruins of their lives; others dealing with a deep sense of disappointment in their lives. Some cannot live their lives at all. Others have destroyed their lives themselves. "To be whole" in the sense of "healthy" and "intact" and "as it should be" is a longing but not a state. Being whole in this sense is a characteristic of the fullness of life, which we only experience in this life for moments at a time. In such moments, we are "completely there"—profoundly present and alert. In such moments, we affirm this life wholeheartedly and are totally engaged; we partake and give fully. In unconditional love, we experience "being whole" in the midst of our tattered, splintered lives.

6. THE LIFE OF THE SOUL

The "Inner Life" of the Soul

The suggestion that the soul is to be holistically understood as the shape of a life and its life story runs counter to Western traditions of spirituality that, since Augustine, have limited the soul to the "inner life" and neglected the outer world of the senses. The "inner life" is rooted in the relationship of individuals to themselves and assumes a dualism of body and soul. The consciousness of a self within individuals' relationships to themselves is an indicator of humans' likeness to God—*imago Dei*—whereas the physical world only includes "traces of God"—*vestigia Dei*. We will attempt to integrate this "inner life" into the entirety of the life lived.

"I desire to know God and the soul," Augustine wrote in his *Soliloquies*. "And nothing more?" the dialogue continues, to which he answers, "Nothing whatever."[10] The path to God is the

---

10 Augustine of Hippo, *The Soliloquies*, trans. Rose E. Cleveland (Altenmünster: Jazzybee Verlag, 2015), 20.

path within. The path within is the path to knowing oneself. It is in the depths of subjectivity that we can experience God. Knowledge of God and knowledge of oneself are inextricably intertwined, as Calvin too was convinced. What is it that connects them? Our likeness to God. The twelfth-century French mystic William of Saint-Thierry wrote a dialogue of God with the soul: "Know yourself, then, to be my image; thus you can know me, whose image you are, and you will find me within you."[11]

The soul's likeness to God served as a sort of mirror in which we could recognize both ourselves and the Creator. Knowledge of oneself is more certain than knowledge of the world, for the self is immediate and requires no mediation via the senses. I can delude myself about everything except about the fact that I delude myself. The soul is understood here as the subject and object of self-knowledge. Hugh of Saint-Victor put it this way: "To ascend to God means, therefore, to enter into oneself, and not only to enter into oneself, but in some ineffable manner to penetrate even into one's depths."[12]

This inner self-transcendence of the soul is possible due to the immanence of God's Spirit in the innermost center of the human soul. This is why it is said that "the path within is the path home."

This spirituality of the "inner life" flowed from medieval mysticism into the Protestant Pietism of the early modern era. Johann Arndt's *True Christianity* (1606–10) and *The Garden of Paradise* (1612) were both extremely popular among seventeenth-century Lutherans. Their Calvinist counterpart was Gerhard Tersteegen's *Spiritual Garden of the Inner Soul* (1729), which recommends, "Close the window to your senses and seek God deep within."

---

11 William of Saint-Thierry, *Exposition on the Song of Songs*, trans. Mother Columba Hart (Spencer, MA: Irish University Press / Cistercian, 1970), 51.

12 Hugh of Saint-Victor, *Hugh of Saint-Victor: Selected Spiritual Writings*, trans. a religious of CSMV (Eugene, OR: Wipf and Stock, 2009), 176.

Tersteegen sought God not only deep within his soul but also beyond creation: "I want the pure Divine—go away, creature! My flesh and heart are wasting away."

He wanted to lose himself in the Divine: "You bottomless sea, in which I lose myself like a single drop."

Since the age of Arndt and Tersteegen, this "inner Christianity" has been considered "true Christianity."

In the words of a popular bygone hymn written by Christian Friedrich Richter in the seventeenth century, "How the inner life of the Christian doth shine, no matter how strong the sun beat down."

A classic description of the inner ascension of the soul to God is Teresa of Avila's *Interior Castle* from 1577. Thomas Merton wrote a modern description of such a spiritual practice in *The Seven Storey Mountain* in 1948. Both authors encounter God in the seventh level of the soul, which suggests that they have internalized the Sabbath of Israel, taking it out of temporal context and into the inner life of the soul.

The trip into the inner life of the soul is preconditioned upon outer isolation and inner silence. Whether in a monastery or in prison, the cell is the place for such meditation. Prisoners confined to the isolation and silence of their cells have no other option than the inner life of their souls. In this inner life, their souls find peace. I was able to observe this process in my correspondence with the inmate Kelly Gissendaner from 2010 until her execution in 2015. She died with the song "Amazing Grace" on her lips.

As the word *spirituality* suggests, it involves a human being moved by the Spirit of God. If an individual waits for the Spirit in this inner life, a "spirituality of the soul" emerges that is to be understood as the relationship of each individual to him or herself. If the Spirit is "poured into our hearts"—as Paul writes in Romans 5:5—it creates a piety of the heart. If the Spirit is poured out "upon all flesh"—as foreseen in the Acts of the Apostles 2:17 in accordance with the prophet Joel—it creates a "spirituality of lived life." In that case, the power of the Spirit is no longer solely "religious" but a life force. If the Spirit is present in all things, as Psalm 104:30 implies, there is a "cosmic spirituality." The widespread spirituality of the inner life is only a small human channel to access the great power of the creative Spirit of the Divine, perhaps the beginning of the redemption of life with all the creatures of the earth.

The Spirit of Life Lived

God created humans in his image: "Male and female he created them." Genesis 1:27 uses the Hebrew term אָדָם or adam in the overarching sense of "[hu]man[kind]" and then goes on to use the plural—"male and female he created them"—in a quite poetic manner. In this account, men and women have the same rights as equal members of this humankind, and yet this "adam" (and its German equivalent, *der Mensch*) is not gender-neutral. Our likeness to God does not begin only in the soul, where in the words of Augustine, "there is no [biological] sex" (ubi sexus nullus est). Humans thus reflect God's image in the community of creation on earth holistically speaking in regards to both body and soul and in the context of human society as man and woman. In the societies in which the ancient Israelites lived, only the kings were considered to resemble the gods. The first biblical account of creation is thus the oldest declaration of human rights of all time. It grants women the same rights as men. It is still revolutionary today.

The body is the temple of the Holy Spirit: "The body is meant . . . for the Lord," and, astonishingly, "the Lord for the body" (1 Cor 6:13); "For you were bought with a price; therefore glorify God in your body" (6:20).

What are we to make of this obvious emphasis placed on the relationship of the body to God? For Plato, it was the *meditatio mortis* that brought certainty regarding the immortality of the soul. For Paul, and then Calvin, it was the *meditatio resurrectionis* that brought certainty regarding the "resurrection of the flesh"—in other words, regarding life. A lived life of love corresponds to the "living God." Humans have bodies endowed

with souls and souls endowed with senses. The body is a manifestation (*Gestalt*) of the soul.

This raises the question of how the soul relates to the world,
in other words, to the physical and sensual aspects of life—
the world as experienced by the soul. This includes human
social relationships. According to Genesis 2:7, "The Lord
God . . . breathed into his nostrils the breath of life; and the man
became a living being." This vividly illustrates how the Spirit
serves as the life-giving force for humankind. Humans thus
perceive this Spirit that flows from God with all the senses of
their own liveliness. Spirituality and vitality do not stand in
opposition: anyone who seeks God must want to live, and anyone who finds the living God wakes to the fullness of life. The
Holy Spirit opens the senses of anyone seized by the divine
Spirit to the miracles of life. We become acutely alert and
attentive—perhaps even "spirited" or "in good spirits."

Humans have five senses. The sense of touch—*sensus
tactus*—is considered the primal sense. We touch and handle
things with our skin, which simultaneously defines and
brings together our inner world with the outer world. We feel
and develop emotions. It is from the skin that envelops our
bodies that the other senses and the brain evolved. All of the
sensual impulses together influence our "sense" of general
(well-)being, which in turn influences our sensual perceptions.
When stricken with acute grief, we become oblivious to everything around us; nothing tastes, smells, or feels good anymore.
The pain tears at our soul. When we are disappointed, we
sometimes become apathetic; we withdraw into ourselves. A
routine, programmatic life makes us numb to other life and
to new things; our soul's function reduces to a bare minimum.

On the other hand, our faith grants us a certain "inner calm"
(or, in German, *Seelenruhe*, literally "a calmness of the soul").
We trust in God and life and do not fear death. We are at ease
with ourselves. The life force of love brings us to life and opens
all our senses. It sparks our interest in the lives of others and
life in fellowship. Love makes us able to be happy, but it also

makes us susceptible to suffering. The life force of hope orients our senses around a life fulfilled. Full of anticipation, we direct our senses to that which awaits us. Our hopes for the life before us wake our senses each new morning.

Assuming we are healthy, we have all five senses available to us, but they are not always equally strong. These senses must be *trained*. We can see but often fail to recognize. We can hear but often fail to listen. Learning *to see* means learning *to look*. It is only when we look that we perceive things for their own sake. In the words of Augustine, our knowledge is limited by the extent of our capacity to love. We hear the sounds of the outer word, but listening must be practiced, as becomes evident in musical instruction.

Judaism, Christianity, and Islam are religions of listening: "Listen, Israel." And it is not always just our ears that hear but sometimes also our heart and soul. When that happens, we are moved or overtaken by surprise.

And finally, social relationships can become alive or spirited or wooden or poisonous. We sometimes say of a mother that she is "the soul of the family." When we feel that we can fundamentally trust and depend on those around us, we deal with each other graciously and charitably. When, however, mistrust dominates these relationships, it mars the atmosphere; we withdraw and prepare ourselves for malicious attacks. It is easy to damage an atmosphere of dependability: every lie does so. It is difficult, however, to salvage the sense of trust. The New Testament cautions over and over again, "Be patient with all of them. See that none of you repays evil for evil, but always seek to do good to one another and to all" (1 Thess 5:14–15). Peace, mutual recognition, justice, and mercy are the "soul" of Christian fellowship and the society in which it desires to flourish and for which it actively works. Solidarity is the "soul" of a society, and societal cohesion is threatened by inequality and restored by social justice.

7. THE DEATH OF A LIVING SOUL

Up until this point I have always spoken of dying but not of death. Now I must explain why: we experience ourselves how life dies—either firsthand or vicariously—but we do not know whether or not those who have had this experience are then "dead." We can thus rightly say that a person has died but not that they are then dead. The word *dead* assumes a final state of which we know nothing.

Our judgments are conditional and relational because they are the judgments of mortals. From our perspective, a beloved individual has died, but from that of the eternal, living God, they are not dead. In fact, "to Him all of them are alive" (Luke 20:38). When we look to Jesus's God, we see the resurrection of Jesus who had died, and because it was God who woke him from the dead, his resurrection is universally effective: "This life was revealed, and we have seen it and testify to it, and declare to you the eternal life that was with the Father and was revealed to us" (1 John 1:2).

The dead will live; thus they are not "dead" in any final sense. It is said that "they are asleep" not because they did not actually die but because the resurrection morning awaits them. We are expected! Because Jesus was awakened from the dead, there is no place more for death, not even for those who die.

What happens when a person dies? Life withdraws from the body; the senses and organs cease their function; their breathing stops; the heart beats no more; the electrical impulses within the brain ebb. The whole disappears, and all that remains are the parts of the body. The corpse is no longer a whole but only a sum of parts. That is why organs can be removed. When the human's connection to the world dies, so does the connection to the self. The dying no longer experience their own death. The connection to God, however, remains, for God is loyal and abides by them in divine love. The divine context of the whole of human life remains. The "soul" as the wholeness of the life's shape (*Lebens-gestalt*) and the story of the life are maintained in this divine context.

The living soul "suffers" the death of the body. It longs for—and calls out to—the living God; it is grieved unto death. It thus suffers the death of its connection to the world, the death of its social connections, and the death of the connection to its own human life. It endures the death of the body, and yet it also transcends it, carried by the divine context of its existence. If we understand life in its entirety to compose the "soul," we can say that "life" suffers the death of the senses and the organs and yet transcends this suffering because its connection to God encompasses and preserves it. Life undergoes death and yet does not die. Our life is both mortal and immortal:

No death can fell us with its fury,
but tears our soul from misery.

(EG 370, verse 8)

This becomes evident in the fellowship with Christ in faith:

Now I will cling forever to Christ, my Savior true;
my Lord will leave me never, whate'er He passes through.
He rends death's iron chain; he breaks through sin and pain;
he shatters hell's dark thrall; I follow Him through all.

(ELW 378, verse 4)

8. THE AWAKENING OF A LIVING SOUL

Symbolically speaking, resurrection has something to do with getting "(back) on one's feet" and walking upright. The German word *Auferstehung* includes the root *steh-*, which means "to stand." *Auferstehung* means then at some level "to stand up again." Someone who is lying on the floor might get back on their feet. And this resurrection—this "getting up"—has to do with "being woken," with "revival" (*Auferweckung*).[13] Such a symbolic awakening happens to one who is asleep. The entire sleeping person is woken. Waking up involves the transition from the unconscious state of sleep to the conscious realm of the alert senses. The "rousing of the soul" is a result of this being woken. All the senses are concentrated on the conscious world.

Without symbols, we speak of the "living soul" and mean the entirety of a life, the life story, and the shape of the life (*Lebensgestalt*). The living soul, like mortal life, can die. If in death the soul experiences the "beginning of [eternal] life," as Dietrich Bonhoeffer suggested in his final words, then its death here corresponds with an awakening there—in the words of the hymn—under the "bright and morning star," that "light of light without beginning," or to be more precise, in the dawn's early light of eternal life. I imagine this to mean that the soul, the life, fades from the body just as its temperature falls, leaving behind a corpse because the soul awakens to eternal life. The process of dying transitions to one of waking; the increasing rigidity here is transformed into lively agility there. For the dying, death does not mean being parted from their lives. Those who die take their entire lives as lived with them in the resurrection to eternal life.

We always associate dying with death, but perhaps it is better to associate death with being woken to everlasting liveliness. When a child is born, we do not lament its departure from the haven of the mother's body, to which it has become accustomed and in which it feels at home, but rather we greet its awakening in a new world that fosters it and demands it become more independent. Christians would thus do well to write the following on their gravestones: "Born on XXX, Resurrected on XXX." After the death of her beloved husband, Marie Luise Kaschnitz composed the following verse:

---

13 Translator's Note: The German word for a religious revival, *Erweckung*, and this "being woken" are also related, just as the most noted revival movements in North America are referred to as the "Great Awakenings."

For a deathbed is no longer a deathbed.
When I am done here
I want to leap with joy
As light as the spirit of the rose.[14]

In our life here, there are two analogies for the death and awakening of a living soul: birth and rebirth.

We no longer remember our own birth. It must have been a "death" of the embryonic life in the womb and an "awakening" in an entirely different world.

The "new birth into a living hope" (1 Pet 1:3) in Christian fellowship is symbolized by baptism, in which the former person dies and a new person is born. In the presence of the resurrected Christ, life is perceived as a new creation: "Everything old has passed away; see, everything has become new!" (2 Cor 5:17). This is how we can imagine the awakening of a deceased person as the dawn of a new life. But the entirety of the life is awakened to rise again. Thus we may anticipate not only the beginning of a new life but also the rectification of this life and all that was injured and died within it. The life is healed as a whole. In the light of that bright and morning star, that light of light without beginning, our entire life story will be present and put to right.

When a child is born, we say that it first sees "the light of day." In the case of the dead being awakened, we can use the expression of Christian Knorr von Rosenroth and speak of an "inexhaustible light"—"that light of light without beginning." That is the primal, uncreated light of God's glory, the light the prophet Isaiah saw in a vision: "Arise, shine; for your light has come, and the glory of the Lord has risen upon you" (Isa 60:1).

The glory of the Lord is portrayed as a sunrise in God's new world. Its light is the primal light of God, the light that "drives out the darkness," whereas the Creator, at the creation

---

14 Marie Luise Kaschnitz, *Gesammelte Werke*, ed. Christian Büttrich and Norbert Miller, vol. 5, *Gedichte* (Frankfurt am Main: Insel, 1985), 517.

of this world, merely "divided" the light created from the "darkness." Christian Orthodox theology holds that Jesus's transfiguration on Mount Tabor was transfiguration in the primal, uncreated light of God: "And while he was praying, the appearance of his face changed, and his clothes became dazzling white" (Luke 9:29).

And Paul envisions Jesus's resurrected body and our awakened life thus: "He will transform our humble bodies that they may be conformed to his glorious body, by the power that also enables him to make all things subject to himself" (Phil 3:21). Death is a portal to the transfiguring light and the process of dying the path therein.

Instead of summoning the courage to acknowledge our finiteness as Fulbert Steffensky recommends, I advocate Friedrich Schleiermacher's position, that we should develop a "sense and taste for the infinite" so that, "in the midst of the finitude," we might "be one with the Infinite and in every moment . . . be eternal." This encompasses the acknowledgment of our finiteness, resistance and capitulation in life, and the courage to die. It is the hope for everlasting life that makes the limitations and restrictions of one's own life bearable. To hope is to anticipate the life to be lived, and the hope of the faithful is an anticipation of eternal life with God. Death is an end and simultaneously a beginning, an end of life in this world and the beginning of life in the world to come. Our "true life" is yet to come. The history of humankind is only the backstory of the real history of true life in the peace of the world's new creation. This new creation is the counterpart to the destruction rampant in this world of death and slaughter.

Christianity exists because this new creation exists. Let us examine the Christian confessions of faith to determine more precisely what this means. Western liturgies most frequently use the Apostles' Creed, which ends in this way:

I believe in the forgiveness of sins,
the resurrection of the dead, and life everlasting.

Forty years ago, this was typically still recited in Germany as "resurrection of the flesh" (*Auferstehung des Fleisches*). In 1971, the Catholic and Protestant Churches in Germany agreed to revise the line to "resurrection of the dead" (*Auferstehung des Toten*). Does this mean the same thing? I think not, for "flesh" emphasizes the bodily resurrection and the resurrection of "everything living," whereas "the dead" places the emphasis on the personal and human resurrection.

The Nicene Creed, which is used in the Orthodox Christian liturgies, includes the line "We look for the resurrection of the dead and the life of the world come."

"Life everlasting" is rendered here as the "life of the world to come." The "resurrection of the dead" is the personal side of eternal life, and "the life of [God's] world to come" is the life in harmony with everything living in the new creation. The Nicene Creed supplies an answer to the question of *where* eternal life takes place. The Apostles' Creed does not address this question, which leads me to believe that we look to the resurrection of the dead in the everlasting life of the world to come.

Should one want to know where the deceased are at present, one has only to think of the life of the coming world of God. The "new creation" includes "a new earth, where righteousness is at home" (2 Pet 3:13), a "new earth" without death and slaughter in the radiance of God's beauty. "Everlasting joy shall be upon their heads" (Isa 35:10).

What does this mean for how we experience the period of our own lifetimes? To think of it as "fleeting" places the focus on our approaching death. Life's ephemeral nature is determined by eternal death. To think, however, of this life as "preliminary" looks to the life to come. Its incipient nature is determined by eternal life.

The incipient nature of time comes first; the ephemeral nature of time is secondary. Birth precedes death. Life supersedes death; life can die, but death cannot live. Life supersedes death, and it can live without death when it is everlasting. Death, however, is intrinsically related to life and cannot kill where there is no life. If death had won, it would no longer exist. Why do we harbor fears of our own deaths? Why do we not speak in death announcements and gravestones of life and this new beginning?

5

Resurrection
The Primal Light Shines in the Midst of Darkness

The brightness of the Light divine
Doth now into our darkness shine;
It breaks upon sin's gloomy night
And makes us children of the light.[1]

(Martin Luther, translation by Charles Kinchin)

I want to close here with some short theological reflections on light and darkness, on created and uncreated light, on the natural night and inhumane darkness. Most especially, however, I will follow Jesus's journey from Gethsemane to Golgotha into "the power of darkness" in order to find the light that shines in the night. It is followed by the prophetic dawn: "Arise, shine; for your light has come" (Isa 60:1). And then by the apostolic morning star: "The night is far gone, the day is near" (Rom 13:12). It deals with that dawn of the "bright and morning star, light of light without beginning," in the paradoxical words

---

1   Martin Luther, "Lord Jesus Christ, All Praise to Thee," in *Hymnal and Liturgies of the Moravian Church*, trans. Charles Kinchin (Bethlehem, PA: Haddon, 1920), 38, https://hymnary.org/hymn/HLMC1920/56.

of the hymn. God's eternity has a dawn in eternal time that itself changes time.

It would appear here that light is always benevolent and darkness always malevolent, but our experience teaches that this is not always true. In wars, firestorms raged through cities, fed by explosives and incendiary devices, leaving countless corpses in their wake. The first atomic explosion over Hiroshima in 1945 cremated a hundred thousand people and was—in the words of Robert Jungk—"brighter than a thousand suns." Darkness, on the other hand, offered some protection. It was in the night that one could flee. In Psalm 139:11, the fugitive from God says, "Surely the darkness shall cover me, and the light around me become night."

But, on the other hand, the "heart of darkness" that Joseph Conrad describes is filled with inhumane abominations, willful blindness, disregard for human rights, torture, imprisonment, mass murder, and war crimes. This darkness also dominated in the gas chambers of Auschwitz. Darkness surrounds atrocities. We take "darkness" to be a symbol for "radical evil," for wantonness and atrocity, and call this age of injustice, violence, and death "dark": "For darkness shall cover the earth, and thick darkness the peoples; but the Lord will arise upon you, and his glory will appear over you" (Isa 60:2).

The "eclipse of God"—also known as "hell"—is treated as Jesus's godforsakenness on the Romans' cross. Only there can one get a sense of it.

1. THE LIGHT OF LIFE

From the perspective of physics, light is electromagnetic energy in a range the human eye can detect. Infrared and ultraviolet light are the parts of the spectrum that border on visible light. They are all created by inner atomic changes and travel at a speed of some 186,000 miles per second. Every different wavelength corresponds to a particular color. Lacking outside influences, light radiates straightly in all directions. Depending on how light is measured, it behaves as a wave or a particle (photon) so that for a time, scientists also spoke of "wavicles."

There is no biological life without sunlight. In the process of photosynthesis, grass, plants, and trees turn light into nutrients and release oxygen into the air. Like all breathing life-forms, humans too live from the intelligence of plants. It is not without cause that the first account of creation in Genesis mentions vegetation no less than four times (1:11–12, 29–30). It is the foundation of all life on earth. The transition from day to night, from light to darkness, is important for all living things and gives rise to the rhythm of life.

Unlike creation myths in the ancient Egyptian and Mesopotamian cultures, the Jewish creation myth suggests that light was created rather than inherently divine: "Then God said, 'Let there be light'; and there was light" (Gen 1:3); "God separated the light from the darkness. God called the light Day, and the darkness he called Night. And there was evening and there was morning, the first day" (1:4–6). The fact that the sun is "merely" part of God's creation makes it an unlikely object of worship. The sun is a "great light" that God has placed in the sky "to rule the day" (1:16). Sunlight is created; it is not the primal, uncreated, divine light. Like everything created by God, it is good and fosters life.

Within the realm of human language across cultures, semantically related words like *light*, *shine*, *sparkle*, *bright*, *flash*, or even *lightning* are used in figurative speech to refer to the recognition and proclamation of knowledge. When someone is "enlightened" or inspired, we say that "a light goes off" (and mean, arguably, that "a light goes on"). The truth is "brought to light." When we understand things, we "see them more clearly." A sudden idea is a "flash of genius" or "a ray of hope." We admire the "radiance" of a perfect "apparition." We speak of the "light of knowledge" or bringing things out "into the light," both of which play a role in "enlightenment." Indeed, the latter concept was applied to a new era that emphasized rational knowledge of the world, an era placed in juxtaposition to the "Dark Ages." "Light" makes our lives "light," whereas darkness

is "oppressing" or "heavy." When the human brain is process-
ing perceptions effectively, we say it is "thinking clearly" or
speak of having "a clear mind," whereas that of which we are
unconscious remains "in the dark."

In religious expression too, light plays an important symbolic role. In the Bible, God is called the "Father of lights"
(Jas 1:17). God "dwells in unapproachable light" (1 Tim 6:16).
The Lord says to Moses, "No one shall see me and live" (Exod
33:20). No human can withstand the radiance of God's glory.
It is as though one were to look straight into the sun: "You are
clothed with honor and majesty, wrapped in light as with a
garment" (Ps 104:1–2). This comparison of the Israelites' God
with the sun has been termed the "solarization of Yahweh."

However, elsewhere the psalms say, "For with you is the
fountain of life; in your light we see light" (Ps 36:9). It must
then be possible for the mortal to discern something of the
divine light. Indeed, the God who reveals himself to humankind, "the Lord" of the Israelites, is "a lamp to my feet and a
light to my path" (119:105). And it is not only along my "life's
path" that the Lord is my light, but also "when I sit in darkness,
the Lord will be a light to me" (Mic 7:8). This is God's descent
into and dwelling in this world—his Shekhinah, in Israel's fate
and also in the lives and fates of each individual, as evidenced
in the psalms.

In the New Testament, this divine light is thus described
as emanating from the incarnate Son of God, Jesus Christ: "In
him was life, and the life was the light of all people" (John 1:4).
Christ is the "true light [that] enlightens everyone coming
into the world" (1:9). In the Gospel of John, Jesus proclaims,
"I am the light of the world. Whoever follows me will never
walk in darkness but will have the light of life" (8:12). As the
"light of the world" and the "light of life," Christ represents
the presence of the Living God among his people, people who
live in darkness. He has come to fill them with the radiance of
his divine love and the enlightenment of the Holy Spirit.

For mortals, the transition to new life is like the transition
from night to day or from darkness to light. It is like waking

up in the morning. The red of dawn heralds the new day: the sun is rising! The grasses and flowers direct their leaves and blossoms to the sun: "The night is far gone, the day is near. Let us then lay aside the works of darkness and put on the armor of light" (Rom 13:12).

God's day is breaking. This beginning gives direction to our life journeys. The beginning was forged with Christ's entrance into this dark world.

2. THE DARKNESS OF DEATH

"God separated the light from the darkness" (Gen 1:4). What is this "separation"? Is it a differentiation like between day and night? How can light have a border? The "black holes" between the stars in the sky are apparently masses so large that light—despite its speed—cannot escape. Physics too then knows of "darkness."

In the biblical account of creation, the formation of the heavens and the earth was threatened by chaos: "Darkness covered the face of the deep" (Gen 1:2). The darkness that God pushed to the side endangered the good creation.

Darkness is also a lack of natural light and might be compared to the deprivation of eyesight—blindness. Just as light gives rise to life, darkness lays waste to all things living. Total darkness is also total coldness. Nothing more moves there. Because darkness means death, it is used as a metaphor for the crimes of humanity. The thief comes "in the night," while "shady characters" sneak around in the shadow of darkness and murderers "shy away from the light." The Gestapo and the KGB routinely came at four in the morning to "pick up" their victims and make them "disappear"—in other words, to murder them.

Among the expressions for evil, the "abyss" and the "eternal night" are some of the most extreme: sin—evil—radical evil—atrocity—degeneracy—inferno—the abyss—the eternal night—eternal death.

The "deeds of darkness" are evil deeds that arise out of "blindness" (i.e., a lack of knowledge or wisdom) and "degeneracy" (i.e., a misdirected will). To "wander in the darkness" is to become a slave to the wrong forces and to engage in lies, betrayal, torture, and murder. When the slaughter of the First World War began in 1914, the English foreign secretary Edward Grey lamented that "the lamps are going out all over Europe, and we shall not see them lit again in our lifetime."

That conflict cost seven million people their lives and led to the Second World War, in which another fifty-five million people died. The "darkness" that fell over the European peoples in the twentieth century, especially over the Germans, brought humankind to the brink of the abyss of self-inflicted annihilation. Terror "from above" in the form of the fascist and Stalinist dictatorships was the signature characteristic of the twentieth century. The "suicide bombers" who seek to take as many lives as possible with their own—terror "from below"— look to be the signature characteristic of the twenty-first century. Many people are struck by a sort of willful blindness, averting their eyes from the threats posed by atomic weapons and the incipient ecological catastrophe that presently encompasses the entire planet. They know not what they do. There are dark times ahead.

The created light of life and darkness held in check, a darkness that nevertheless breaks through and kills parts of creation, that is the image of darkness as found in the biblical traditions. There is, however, an even darker darkness: the eclipse of God. What happens when God regrets not only having created humankind but even all of creation? What happens when God turns his back on creation? Then the created light sinks into eternal darkness and all that is fades into eternal nothingness. Rather than ending in everlasting life, it ends in everlasting death. The faith that understands creation as something distinct from the Creator leaves open the possibility that God might turn his back on that creation. Something unexpected happened during Christmas 2003, when a sort of apocalyptic eclipse fell upon St. Peter's Cathedral. Pope John Paul II suddenly saw the night of godforsakenness descending upon the world: "Following upon hunger and violence, there is a greater tragedy: a subsidence of hope. God is no longer revealing himself. He seems to have closed himself up in heaven, repulsed by the depravity of humankind. Now we feel abandoned and lonely without peace or salvation. Humankind has been left to its own devices and feels lost and overwhelmed by fear." (*Der Spiegel*, Christmas issue, 2003)

The "realm of darkness" itself has no substance; it exists only in the negation of good, of light, and of life. That is why the realms of darkness collapsed without any great ado. Their flimsy facades had been built on fear.

3. JESUS'S PATH INTO THE DARKNESS

According to the Gospel of Luke, when Jesus was taken prisoner in the Garden of Gethsemane, he told his captors, "This is your hour, and the power of darkness!" (Luke 22:53). This scene in Gethsemane is the most astonishing story about Jesus in all of the Gospels. He who has healed many sick people, who has proclaimed the coming of God's kingdom, appears startled, hesitant, apprehensive, and eager to evade his fate. What scares him? What is he afraid of? Why does the evangelist chronicle his weakness? What is meant by "the reproach of Christ" (Heb 11:26, KJV)?

According to the oldest gospel account, that of Mark, Jesus "took with him Peter and James and John, and began to be distressed and agitated. And he said to them, 'I am deeply grieved, even to death; remain here, and keep awake'" (Mark 14:33–34). The later account in Luke similarly describes the scene: "In his anguish he prayed more earnestly, and his sweat became like great drops of blood falling down on the ground" (Luke 22:44). The reason, according to the Gospels, was because "the Son of Man is betrayed into the hands of sinners" (Matt 26:45; Mark 14:41). There was, however, also another factor at play: Jesus pleads with God, to whom he refers in this hour of distress as "Father," to "remove this cup from me" if God so wills (Mark 14:36; Matt 26:39; Luke 22:42). Nevertheless, God his "father" did not heed this petition from his "beloved son" (Mark 1:11), and God even remained silent. Jesus's statement, however, that "not my will but yours be done," shows that he did not agree with the will of God. He denies his own will to follow that of God. Wracked with anguish and apprehension, his soul in despair, beads of nervous sweat running down his face, Jesus envisions his path into the heart of darkness. Composers have more accurately recognized Jesus's dread and terror in that moment than some theologians in their works of dogmatic Christology. Paul Gerhardt's classic hymn "O Haupt voll Blut und Wunden," which Johann Sebastian Bach partially included in his *St Matthew Passion*, notes not only Christ's suffering but also his fear:

> When my heart is filled with dread
> and terror afflicts my head
> you pull me from this torment
> because, despite fear and pain, you went.

(EG 85, verse 9)

Jesus goes through all the shades of darkness: betrayal, disownment, being abandoned by those around him, imprisonment, torture, and "slow death" on the Romans' cross. The religious leaders of his own people condemn him as a "blasphemer" (Matt 26:65), the Roman occupation forces crucify him as an anti-imperial "insurgent," and his God abandons him to die alone—godforsaken (Mark 15:34). God was eclipsed on the cross at Golgotha, as symbolized in a solar eclipse: "When it was noon, darkness came over the whole land until three in the afternoon" (Mark 15:33). Paul even viewed Jesus as having incurred God's curse on our behalf: "Christ redeemed us from the curse of the law by becoming a curse for us" (Gal 3:13). That is Jesus's "descent into hell," into the eternal nights and everlasting death, as Luther and Calvin understood it. Jesus Christ thereby becomes a brother to those damned in this world, to those who live in some kind of darkness of their own. The "Son of Man" becomes a mortal brother to victims of the darkness. The godforsaken Son of God stands shoulder to shoulder with all those who feel godforsaken.

4. JESUS'S RESURRECTION THROUGH THE ETERNAL LIGHT

The account of Christ's transfiguration in the Gospel of Matthew (17:1–8) gives us some idea of what it might be like to be resurrected in God's divine light: "And he was transfigured before them, and his face shone like the sun, and his clothes became dazzling white. Suddenly . . . a bright cloud overshadowed them, and from the cloud a voice said, 'This is my Son, the Beloved; with him I am well pleased; listen to him!' . . . Jesus ordered them, 'Tell no one about the vision until after the Son of Man has been raised from the dead'" (Matt 17:1–9). It is the light of the burning thorn bush of Moses. It is the light that surrounded the prophet Isaiah when he saw God (Isa 6). It is the primal "uncreated light of knowledge" sought by the monks on Mount Athos.

No one has seen it. There is no one who has witnessed this process. From the very beginning, however, the apostles and the women who had been closest to Jesus used the eschatological symbol of "having been woken" (*Auferweckung*) and "having been raised" (*Auferstehung*) to describe what happened between Jesus's death on the cross and his "apparitions" in his new being. While interpretations of his death varied, his "having been woken from the dead" has consistently been seen as the very beginning of the Christian faith. This expression represents an enormous shift away from Jewish expectations. According to the prophecy of Daniel 12:2, all the deceased shall be roused simultaneously on the last day to face God's judgment, which shall send "some to everlasting life, and some to shame and everlasting contempt." From the point of Jesus's resurrection, however, Christians have understood his resurrection to represent the first instance of someone having been raised "from the dead." Christ's resurrection is,

furthermore, not thought to represent an exception or anticipation of some later event but rather to begin a process of resurrection as described by Paul in 1 Corinthians 15:20–28. This
process of resurrection begins with the crucified, deceased
Jesus and shall in the end include all of creation. Rather than
an ambiguous resurrection intended to pave the way for the
Last Judgment, this is an awakening in the everlasting life
in the world of God to come: "Death has been swallowed up in
victory" (1 Cor 15:54). Hell has been destroyed. Darkness is
driven out by eternal light. In the words of the Sunday liturgy
commonly used in the Orthodox Christian churches,

> You have shattered the gates of Hades, O Lord,
> and by Your death, You have destroyed the dominion of Death,
> delivering mankind from corruption,
> granting the world life, incorruption, and great mercy.[2]

Because this "reawakening" of the resurrection depends
on the light of morning, we can envision what it might look
like: like a bolt of lightning, the primal, uncreated light of God
strikes in the heart of darkness. In the midst of great darkness,
God arises over the deceased Jesus, and his glory appears over
him (Isa 60:2). Because light means life, eternal light means
eternal life. Jesus, having been raised from the dead, will be the
"light of life." This light radiates out from him over the realm
of the dead, over the realm of the living, and over the heavens. This is the "dawn of eternity" (*Morgenglanz der Ewigkeit*).
The separation of light and dark that marked the beginning
of creation is rescinded: "Now all is filled with light," as the
Eastern Churches sing in the Paschal Canon. Christ's reawakening is also God's resurrection, and this is like a sunrise. God
breaks his silence and shines through the darkness; he answers
Jesus's cry of anguished abandonment on the cross with the
beginning of the new creation of the world. At Easter we sing,

---

2   Fr. Joseph Irvin, *Great Vespers*, Orthodox Service Books, Number 5 (self-pub., Lulu Press,
    2019).

Were Christ not arisen,
then death were still our prison.
Now, with him to life restored

(ELW 372)

And

The sun, the earth, all of creation,
afflicted as it was,
rejoices now in harmony,
for this is the day of Christ's victory

(EG 106, English translation EYG)

The wonderful Orthodox Easter icon shows the resurrected Christ as the head of a new humankind, pulling Adam and Eve up out the world of death with both hands. In the Easter liturgy commonly used in the Orthodox Christian churches, it is sung,

Now all is filled with light;
Heaven and earth, and the lower regions.
Let all creation celebrate the rising of Christ.
In Him we are established.[3]

5. "LIGHT EVERLASTING ENTERS THERE"

The resurrection of Christ is the reason for the recognition of the divine incarnation in him. The end illuminates the beginning. Paul recognizes that Jesus "was declared to be Son of God . . . by resurrection from the dead" (Rom 1:4). The evangelist Mark describes Jesus's relationship to God in his account of how John the Baptist baptized Christ: "And a voice came

---

3   Fr. Joseph Irvin, *Memorial, Funeral & Burial Services*, Orthodox Service Books, Number 7 (self-pub., Lulu Press, 2019).

from heaven, 'You are my Son, the Beloved; with you I am well pleased'" (Mark 1:11). Matthew and Luke both incorporate Jesus's relationship to God in their stories of his birth.

It is the Gospel of John that first locates Jesus Christ's origins in heaven: "In the beginning was the Word. . . . In him was life, and the life was the light of all people. The light shines in the darkness, and the darkness did not overcome it" (John 1:1, 4–5). And the Jesus of the Gospel of John declares accordingly, "I am the light of the world. Whoever follows me will never walk in darkness but will have the light of life" (John 8:12).

This means that the earthly Jesus Christ is only the light that shines in the darkness but not yet the light that drives out darkness entirely. For those who believe and follow Christ, the "light of life" shines in the dark world of death. They are "children of the light" even in dark times: you "shine as lights in the world" (Phil 2:15 KJV); "For it is the God who said, 'Let light shine out of darkness,' who has shone in our hearts to give the light of the knowledge of the glory of God" (2 Cor 4:6).

What is the nature of this light that shines in the darkness? It is a divine light in mortal light. In Jesus, this light is simultaneously eternal and temporal. It is a light that both reveals to us the glory of God in Jesus's face and shines in our own lives. The Nicene Creed extols the divine light in Jesus: "God from God, Light from Light, true God from true God." But it also says that Jesus carried this divine light to the heart of darkness so that the proclamation of Psalm 139:12 became reality:

> Even the darkness is not dark to you;
> the night is as bright as the day.

The light that shines out of the darkness is not the light that was "separated" from the darkness but rather a harbinger of the light that will banish darkness forever. There is a fitting passage in Isaiah: during their time in exile, far from home, strangers among strangers, the prisoners of the Israelites, come to the prophet and ask, "'Sentinel, what of the night? Sentinel, what of the night?' The sentinel says: 'Morning comes, and also the night. If you will inquire, inquire; come back again.'" (Isa 21:11–12). Paul, however, Christ's witness, proclaimed, "The night is far gone, the day is near. Let us then lay aside the works of darkness and put on the armor of light" (Rom 13:12). Heraclitus said, "The waking have one common world, but the sleeping turn aside each into a world of his own."[4] This holds true for those who have been woken by the "light of life." Martin Luther's Christmas hymn "Lord Jesus Christ, All Praise to Thee" includes a line about our being "children of the light." The term might just as well be applied to those who have already been resurrected. They are beacons of hope, a reminder that "the Light divine" will break "upon sin's gloomy night." That light "doth now into our darkness shine," and in the end, it will banish darkness from creation forevermore, until we stand together in the light.

---

4   English translation taken from "Heraclitus," Wikipedia, May 17, 2020, https://en
.wikipedia.org/w/index.php?title=Heraclitus&oldid=957149848.

Works Cited

Alighieri, Dante. *The Divine Comedy of Dante Alighieri*. Vol. 2. Translated by Courtney Langdon. Cambridge, MA: Harvard University Press, 1920.

Augustine of Hippo. *The Soliloquies*. Translated by Rose E. Cleveland. Altenmünster: Jazzybee Verlag, 2015.

Campbell, Joseph. *The Mysteries*. Princeton, NJ: Princeton University Press, 1978.

Carver, Matthew. "Wir Wollen Alle Fröhlich Sein." HYMNOGLYPT (blog), April 25, 2014. http://matthaeusglyptes.blogspot.com/2014/04/wir-wollen-alle-frohlich-sein.html.

Descartes, René. *Descartes: Meditations on First Philosophy: With Selections from the Objections and Replies*. Edited and translated by John Cottingham. 2nd ed. Cambridge: Cambridge University Press, 2017.

Eichendorff, Josef Karl Benedikt von. "Moonlit Night." Translated by Walter A. Aue, 2008. LiederNet Archive. https://www.lieder.net/lieder/get_text.html?TextId=38193.

Evangelical Lutheran Worship. Pew edition. Minneapolis: Augsburg Fortress, 2006.

Goethe, Johann Wolfgang von. "Welcome and Farewell." In *Selected Poems*, edited and translated by Christopher Middleton, 9–11. Princeton, NJ: Princeton University Press, 1994.

Goodrich, Charles Augustus. *The Universal Traveller: Designed to Introduce Readers at Home to an Acquaintance with the Arts, Customs, and Manners of the Principal Modern Nations on the Globe*. 4th ed. New York: Collins, Sheldon, and Converse, 1838.

Gruchy, John W. de, ed. *The Cambridge Companion to Dietrich Bonhoeffer*. Cambridge: Cambridge University Press, 1999.

"Heraclitus." Wikipedia, May 17, 2020. https://en.wikipedia.org/w/index.php?title=Heraclitus&oldid=957149848.

Hesse, Hermann. *Magister Ludi*. Translated by Mervyn Savill. London: Aldus, 1949.

Hugh of Saint-Victor. *Hugh of Saint-Victor: Selected Spiritual Writings*. Translated by a Religious of CSMV. Eugene, OR: Wipf and Stock, 2009.

Hymnary. "Paul Gerhardt." Accessed May 3, 2020. https://hymnary.org/person/Gerhardt_Paul.

Irvin, Joseph. *Great Vespers*. Orthodox Service Books, Number 5. Self-published, Lulu Press, 2019.

———. *Memorial, Funeral & Burial Services*. Orthodox Service Books, Number 7. Self-published, Lulu Press, 2019.

Kaschnitz, Marie Luise. *Gesammelte Werke*, Vol. 5, *Gedichte*. Edited by Christian Büttrich and Norbert Miller. 7 vols. Frankfurt am Main: Insel, 1985.

———. *Selected Later Poems of Marie Luise Kaschnitz*. Translated by Lisel Mueller. Princeton, NJ: Princeton University Press, 1980.

King, Karen L. *The Gospel of Mary of Magdala: Jesus and the First Woman Apostle*. Santa Rosa, CA: Polebridge Press, 2003.

Luther, Martin. "Lord Jesus Christ, All Praise to Thee." In *Hymnal and Liturgies of the Moravian Church*. Translated by Charles Kinchin. No. 56, 38. Bethlehem, PA, 1920. https://hymnary.org/hymn/HLMC1920/56.

———. "A Sermon on Preparing to Die (1519)." In *Devotional Writings*, Vol. 1, Luther's Works 42. Edited by Martin O. Dietrich and Helmut T. Lehmann. Translated by Martin H. Bertram. Minneapolis: Fortress, 1969.

———. "Sermons on the Second Epistle of St. Peter." In *The Catholic Epistles*, Luther's Works 30. Edited by Jaroslav Pelikan and Walter A.

Hansen. Translated by Martin H. Bertram. St. Louis: Concordia, 2007.

Mead, G. R. S., trans. *Pistis Sophia: A Gnostic Gospel*. San Diego: Book Tree, 2006.

Moltmann, Jürgen. *The Coming of God: Christian Eschatology*. Translated by Margaret Kohl. Minneapolis: Fortress, 2005.

——. *In the End—the Beginning: The Life of Hope*. Translated by Margaret Kohl. Minneapolis: Fortress, 2004.

Moltmann-Wendel, Elisabeth. *Autobiography*. Translated by John Bowden. London: SCM Press, 1997.

——. *The Women around Jesus*. New York: Crossroad, 1990. http://archive.org/details/womenaroundjesus0000unse.

Pagels, Elaine. *Beyond Belief: The Secret Gospel of Thomas*. New York: Random House, 2003.

Reid, William. *The Praise Book*. London: James Nisbet & Company, 1872.

Ring, Bonnie. *Women Who Knew Jesus*. Ishpeming, MI: BookVenture, 2017.

Schiller, Friedrich. *Wallenstein's Camp*. Translated by Theodor Wirgman. London: David Nutt, 1871.

Seper, Franjo Cardinal. "Letter on Certain Questions Concerning Eschatology." Sacred Congregation for the Doctrine of the Faith, May 17, 1979. http://www.vatican.va/roman_curia/congregations/cfaith/documents/rc_con_cfaith_doc_19790517_escatologia_en.html.

William of Saint-Thierry. *Exposition on the Song of Songs*. Translated by Mother Columba Hart. Spencer, MA: Irish University Press / Cistercian, 1970.

Zink, Jörg. *Erinnerungen: Sieh nach den Sternen—gib acht auf die Gassen*. 2nd ed. Stuttgart: Kreuz, 1992.

Bibliography

Alighieri, Dante. *The Divine Comedy of Dante Alighieri*. Vol. 2. Translated by Courtney Langdon. Cambridge, MA: Harvard University Press, 1920.

Althaus, Paul. *Die letzten Dinge: Lehrbuch der Eschatologie*. Gütersloh: Bartelsmann, 1957.

Augustine of Hippo. *The Soliloquies*. Translated by Rose E. Cleveland. Altenmünster: Jazzybee Verlag, 2015.

Campbell, Joseph. *The Mysteries*. Princeton, NJ: Princeton University Press, 1978.

Carver, Matthew. "Wir Wollen Alle Fröhlich Sein." HYMNOGLYPT (blog), April 25, 2014. http://matthaeusglyptes.blogspot.com/2014/04/wir-wollen-alle-frohlich-sein.html.

Demetrios (archbishop). "Encyclical for Holy Pascha." Greek Orthodox Archdiocese of America, May 5, 2013. https://www.goarch.org/-/encyclical-of-archbishop-demetrios-for-holy-pascha-may-5-2013?inheritRedirect=true.

Descartes, René. *Descartes: Meditations on First Philosophy: With Selections from the Objections and Replies*. Edited and translated by John Cottingham. 2nd ed. Cambridge: Cambridge University Press, 2017.

Eckstein, Hans-Joachim, and Michael Welker, eds. *Die Wirklichkeit der Auferstehung*. Neukirchen-Vluyn: Neukirchener Theologie, 2002.

Eichendorff, Josef Karl Benedikt von. "Moonlit Night." Translated by Walter A. Aue, 2008. LiederNet Archive. https://www.lieder.net/lieder/get_text.html?TextId=38193.

Evangelical Lutheran Worship. Pew edition. Minneapolis: Augsburg Fortress, 2006.

Gerhardt, Paul. "Ah Wounded Head." In *German Poetry: With the English Versions of the Best Translators*, edited by H. E. Goldschmidt, translated by Catherine Winkworth, 417–23. London: Williams and Norgate, 1869.

Goethe, Johann Wolfgang von. "Welcome and Farewell." In *Selected Poems*, edited and translated by Christopher Middleton, 9–11. Princeton, NJ: Princeton University Press, 1994.

Goodrich, Charles Augustus. *The Universal Traveller: Designed to Introduce Readers at Home to an Acquaintance with the Arts, Customs, and Manners of the Principal Modern Nations on the Globe*. 4th ed. New York: Collins, Sheldon, and Converse, 1838.

Grabmann, Martin. *Die Grundgedanken des heiligen Augustinus über Seele und Gott*. 2nd ed. Darmstadt: Wissenschaftliche Buchgesellschaft, 1967.

Greshake, Gisbert, and Jacob Kremer. *Resurrectio mortuorum: zum theologischen Verständnis der leiblichen Auferstehung*. Darmstadt: Wissenschaftliche Buchgesellschaft, 1986.

Gruchy, John W. de, ed. *The Cambridge Companion to Dietrich Bonhoeffer*. Cambridge: Cambridge University Press, 1999.

"Heraclitus." Wikipedia, May 17, 2020. https://en.wikipedia.org/w/index.php?title=Heraclitus&oldid=957149848.

Hesse, Hermann. *Magister Ludi*. Translated by Mervyn Savill. London: Aldus, 1949.

Hugh of Saint-Victor. *Hugh of Saint-Victor: Selected Spiritual Writings*. Translated by a Religious of CSMV. Eugene, OR: Wipf and Stock, 2009.

Hymnary. "Paul Gerhardt." Accessed May 3, 2020. https://hymnary.org/person/Gerhardt_Paul.

Irvin, Joseph. *Great Vespers*. Orthodox Service Books, Number 5. Self-published, Lulu Press, 2019.

———. *Memorial, Funeral & Burial Services*. Orthodox Service Books, Number 7. Self-published, Lulu Press, 2019.

Janowski, Bernd, and Christoph Schwöbel, eds. *Gott—Seele—Welt: Interdisziplinäre Beiträge zur Rede von der Seele*. Neukirchen-Vluyn: Neukirchener Theologie, 2013.

Janssen, Claudia. *Endlich lebendig: Die Kraft der Auferstehung erfahren*. Freiburg: Kreuz Verlag, 2013.

Kaschnitz, Marie Luise. *Gesammelte Werke*, Vol. 5, *Gedichte*. Edited by Christian Büttrich and Norbert Miller. 7 vols. Frankfurt am Main: Insel, 1985.

——. *Selected Later Poems of Marie Luise Kaschnitz*. Translated by Lisel Mueller. Princeton, NJ: Princeton University Press, 1980.

King, Karen L. *The Gospel of Mary of Magdala: Jesus and the First Woman Apostle*. Santa Rosa, CA: Polebridge Press, 2003.

Knecht, Gotthold, ed. *Ich lebe und ihr sollt auch leben: Texte zur Auferstehung*. Nürtingen: Denkhaus, 2018.

Kuhn, Johannes. *Wir werden erwartet am letzten Ufer*. Stuttgart: Quell, 1992.

Luther, Martin. "Lord Jesus Christ, All Praise to Thee." In *Hymnal and Liturgies of the Moravian Church*. Translated by Charles Kinchin. No. 56, 38. Bethlehem, PA, 1920. https://hymnary.org/hymn/HLMC1920/56.

——. "A Sermon on Preparing to Die (1519)." In *Devotional Writings*, Vol. 1, Luther's Works 42. Edited by Martin O. Dietrich and Helmut T. Lehmann. Translated by Martin H. Bertram. Minneapolis: Fortress, 1969.

——. "Sermons on the Second Epistle of St. Peter." In *The Catholic Epistles*, Luther's Works 30. Edited by Jaroslav Pelikan and Walter A. Hansen. Translated by Martin H. Bertram. St. Louis: Concordia, 2007.

Mead, G. R. S., trans. *Pistis Sophia: A Gnostic Gospel*. San Diego: Book Tree, 2006.

Moltmann, Jürgen. *The Coming of God: Christian Eschatology*. Translated by Margaret Kohl. Minneapolis: Fortress, 2005.

——. *In the End—the Beginning: The Life of Hope*. Translated by Margaret Kohl. Minneapolis: Fortress, 2004.

Moltmann-Wendel, Elisabeth. *Autobiography*. Translated by John Bowden. London: SCM Press, 1997.

———. *The Women around Jesus*. New York: Crossroad, 1990. http://archive.org/details/womenaroundjesus0000unse.

Pagels, Elaine. *Beyond Belief: The Secret Gospel of Thomas*. New York: Random House, 2003.

Reid, William. *The Praise Book*. London: James Nisbet & Company, 1872.

Ring, Bonnie. *Women Who Knew Jesus*. Ishpeming, MI: BookVenture, 2017.

Schiller, Friedrich. *Wallenstein's Camp*. Translated by Theodor Wirgman. London: David Nutt, 1871.

Schleiermacher, Friedrich. "On Religion: Speeches to Its Cultured Despisers." In *A History of Christianity*, edited by Clyde Manschreck, 2:335–41. Grand Rapids, MI: Baker, 1981. https://pages.uoregon.edu/sshoemak/323/texts/schleiermacher.htm.

Seper, Franjo Cardinal. "Letter on Certain Questions Concerning Eschatology." Sacred Congregation for the Doctrine of the Faith, May 17, 1979. http://www.vatican.va/roman_curia/congregations/cfaith/documents/rc_con_cfaith_doc_19790517_escatologia_en.html.

William of Saint-Thierry. *Exposition on the Song of Songs*. Translated by Mother Columba Hart. Spencer, MA: Irish University Press / Cistercian, 1970.

Zink, Jörg. *Erinnerungen: Sieh nach den Sternen—gib acht auf die Gassen*. 2nd ed. Stuttgart: Kreuz, 1992.

Index